"I spent 16 years working for the FBI, CIA and ATF, teaching thousands of law enforcement agents how to decipher fact from fiction. Now, I teach millions in the public how to do the same. In his amazing new book, Scott shows you how to read, understand, and surround yourself with people who will help make both your personal and your professional life very fulfilling and very prosperous."

—JANINE DRIVER, New York Times bestselling author of
You Say More Than You Think and *You Can't Lie to Me*

"This book is both smart and wise. Through multiple case studies, Scott shows us how caring, thoughtful leaders understand that their values and character will, in the long run, forge their careers and lives into a productive and happy future. Parents, students, and those of us trying to become better leaders should all consider this an important read."

—DON BISHOP, Associate Vice President of Undergraduate Enrollment,
University of Notre Dame

"It took about three paragraphs for me to get completely hooked by Scott Deming's new book. With a distinctive and compelling perspective on what matters most in business, this book will make a positive difference in your work and your life."

—JOE CALLOWAY, author of *Be The Best At What Matters Most*

"Scott has been successful for years by following a practice of connecting values to his daily life, whether it's leading a business, sharing his message, or connecting people to the important cause of child safety. This book will quickly connect with you and open your eyes to the true meaning and formula for lasting success."

—KATE CARR, CEO, Safe Kids Worldwide

"I've worked with Scott Deming over the years and have personally seen his processes turn our bottom line into profits. His new book is laced with ideas and steps to help you create a truly profitable and powerful network of likeminded people for your personal and professional life."

—JIM D'AGOSTINO, Vice President, Trane Heating & Cooling

SCOTT DEMING

POWERED PURPOSE BY

Identify Your Values, Discover Your Purpose,
and Build Success for Life!

GREENLEAF
BOOK GROUP PRESS

Published by Greenleaf Book Group Press
Austin, Texas
www.greenleafbookgroup.com

Distributed by Greenleaf Book Group

For ordering information or special discounts for bulk purchases, please contact
Greenleaf Book Group at PO Box 91869, Austin, TX 78709, 512.891.6100.

Design and composition by Greenleaf Book Group
Cover design by Greenleaf Book Group

Publisher's Cataloging-In-Publication Data
Deming, Scott.
    Powered by purpose : identify your values, discover your purpose, and build
success for life! / Scott Deming.—First edition.
    pages ; cm
    Issued also as an ebook.
    Includes bibliographical references.
    ISBN: 978-1-62634-125-8
    1. Deming, Scott. 2. Success in business—Psychological aspects. 3. Self-
actualization (Psychology) 4. Values. 5. Leadership. 6. Corporate culture. I. Title.

HF5386 .D46 2014
650.1   2014938073

Part of the Tree Neutral® program, which offsets the number of trees
consumed in the production and printing of this book by taking
proactive steps, such as planting trees in direct proportion to the
number of trees used: www.treeneutral.com.

TreeNeutral

Printed in the United States of America on acid-free paper

19 20 21 22 23 24   11 10 9 8 7 6 5 4 3 2

First Edition

To Amaya
Thank you for the daily inspiration.
Oh, how we miss you.

CONTENTS

ACKNOWLEDGMENTS ~ *ix*

PROLOGUE ~ *1*

INTRODUCTION ~ *9*

CHAPTER 1: *Define Success in Terms of Values, Then Lead* ~ *15*

CHAPTER 2: *Identify Your Values* ~ *21*

CHAPTER 3: *Determine the Source of Your Values* ~ *33*

CHAPTER 4: *How I Uncovered My Purpose* ~ *43*

CHAPTER 5: *Pursuing Your Purpose Through Critical Thinking* ~ *57*

CHAPTER 6: *Achieving Your Purpose Through Refined Critical Thinking* ~ *67*

CHAPTER 7: *Surround Yourself With People Who Share Your Values, Believe in Your Purpose, and Aren't Afraid to Speak Their Minds* ~ *79*

CHAPTER 8: *A Culture Flourishes Around Shared Values* ~ *91*

CHAPTER 9: *How to Build a Flourishing Culture Around Your Values* ~ *105*

CHAPTER 10: *Do Only What Supports Your Values and Achieves Your Purpose* ~ *121*

CHAPTER 11: *The Heart of Getting Others Involved in Your Purpose* ~ *137*

CHAPTER 12: *Good, Better, and Best Ways to Get Others on Board to Achieve Your Purpose* ~ *151*

CHAPTER 13: *To Promote Your Purpose, Create Intrigue* ~ *165*

CHAPTER 14: *Your Values and Purpose Can Cover the World* ~ *179*

NOTES ~ *195*

INDEX ~ *207*

ABOUT THE AUTHOR ~ *214*

ACKNOWLEDGMENTS

First and foremost, I wish to thank and acknowledge my wife Deborah, for her unwavering support for this book. This project, like every project in my life would not see fruition if it weren't for my dedicated partner. I love you.

A very special thank you goes to Mia Wood for her wonderful research and editing skills. She is tireless and has the patience of a saint–a necessary attribute when working with me.

I greatly appreciate the invaluable contributions from Dennis Mehiel and Howard Schmidt, who both participated in my business podcast, and allowed me to use our conversations and their brilliant insights. Many will learn from these two gentlemen.

I want to thank The Davey Tree Company for allowing me to use a treasured document within these pages that has been their corporate compass for so many years. Hopefully, it will guide others as well.

Thank you, Greenleaf Book Group! What a wonderful experience it has been working with such a group of professionals. Your guidance and patience is so greatly appreciated. From design to editing to distribution, it has been top shelf the entire way. Thank you Alan Grimes, Brian Phillips, Amber Hales, Hobbs Allison, Steve Elizalde, Linda O'Doughda, Thom Lemmons, Joan Tapper, Rachael Brandenburg, Emilie Lyons, and Chantel Stull. What a team!

Finally, I simply wish to thank all of the companies and individuals highlighted throughout this book who serve as a source of inspiration and example. I am always in awe of those who possess the unique combination of brilliance, compassion, and empathy. It is these people who let their values guide them to their purpose that I will forever look up to and be grateful for.

PROLOGUE

It was approximately 6:30 on the evening of September 11, 2012. I had just sat down in an airport terminal restaurant and taken a bite of my sandwich and a sip of beer when my wife called.

"Hi, honey!" I said happily.

"Hi!" Deb said. "I'm just calling to say I'm on my way to Philly to pick you up."

I had just finished a half-day training program for AT&T in Dallas, Texas, and was awaiting my next flight to Philadelphia. My wife, Debbie, and I had plans to meet there and then drive to Atlantic City, where I had another speaking engagement for a bank group the following afternoon. We were going to spend an extra day after my event to have some fun.

"I can't wait to see you," I said. "I'll call you as soon as the plane touches down."

We hung up. Less than thirty minutes later, as I stood in line to board the plane, my phone rang again. Before I had a chance to say anything, I heard my wife's frantic screams. I immediately thought she was hurt.

"Slow down!" I yelled. "What's wrong?"

She continued screaming and rambling, as I tried desperately to understand what she was saying. Finally, I heard it. "Amaya's dead!" she screamed. "She's dead!"

I was dumbfounded. This was impossible. Our granddaughter, not yet three years old, could not be dead. "What? What are you talking about?"

She screamed again, "Amaya's dead!"

I stood there, stunned and numb as people moved past me onto the plane. That was the longest, worst moment of my entire life, which turned into the longest, worst week I've ever experienced.

Our granddaughter Amaya, just one month shy of turning three years old, died suddenly and tragically. She was with her mom, our daughter Danielle, at home. They had just finished dinner. Her mom was cleaning up in the kitchen and Amaya asked if they could watch *Madagascar*.

"Sure" her mom told her. "Go get the movie, and Mommy will be right in."

Everything was going as it normally did, night after night. Danielle would quickly do the dishes, and Amaya would pick out a DVD from the drawer of the television stand. Except, on this particular night, Amaya decided she wanted to put the movie into the DVD player herself. It was sitting on top of a large tube-style television, which was sitting on the television stand. She pulled the bottom drawer of the stand out, stood on it to reach the DVD player, and the television came down on top of her, killing her instantly. Our lives will never be the same.

The day of her funeral, we all painted our fingernails hot pink. This was to honor Amaya, as hot pink was her favorite color. She wore pink ribbons, pink clothes, pink shoes, and, of course, pink nail polish. So the decision was made that the ladies would paint all of their nails, while the guys painted just their pinky. It was a wonderful tribute to Amaya.

About one month after the funeral, my good friend Wayne Irons came into town, and we went to lunch. He had joined in and put pink polish on his pinky, and he told me that he left it on after the funeral, and that people kept asking him why he wore it. Wayne is a tall, muscular, rather intimidating-looking man and a successful executive—highly professional. To see someone like him wearing pink nail polish instantly begs the question, "What's up?" Whenever someone asked him about his pink pinky, he told the story about Amaya. And the story invariably drew a gasp from his horror-stricken listener.

As Wayne told me about his repeated experiences, a plan started forming in my mind. "I'm going to paint my pinky pink again," I said. "People will ask me why I'm wearing it—but I don't want gasps, and I don't want sympathy. All I want is to tell my story. I want to get a conversation going." I knew this was not just Amaya's story but also an account of how this same exact type of accident happens every eleven to fourteen days in the US alone.[1]

That's a shocking figure, but it's true. Every eleven to fourteen days, a television or other piece of furniture falls and kills a child. I decided I would tell this story with a single purpose in mind: to prevent things like that from occurring again. Shortly after Amaya's death, I started researching how this terrible event could happen in an age of child-safety awareness. Products promoting child safety abound—everything from electrical outlet covers to cabinet locks and baby gates. Yet it is staggering how frequently toddlers are killed by preventable accidents. That knowledge led me to another decision.

It wasn't long after Amaya's death that my wife and I were sitting at home, still overcome with grief and stunned by disbelief. We were sad, confused, and angry—no, we were really pissed off! We couldn't understand it. The only thing we could really get our heads around was the fact that we didn't want anyone to ever go through what we were experiencing.

I looked at my wife and said, "We need to do something to keep this from happening. We need to protect children and save other parents and grandparents from the pain we're going through."

To save lives, Deborah and I started a foundation called Safe and Sound with Amaya.[2] From the outset, our goal has been to raise awareness of the dangers that lie in and around otherwise safe homes. And we're getting the word out in many different ways. I don't walk around lecturing about the subject on a day-to-day basis, nor do I ever bring it up to anyone sitting or standing next to me. I simply wear my pink nail polish, along with my pink bracelet, and just wait for the curious person near me to ask the inevitable question, "Do you mind me asking you a question? Why are you wearing pink nail polish on your pinky?"

Then I say, "I wear it so you would ask me why I wear it. Here's why." I tell my story, educate people, send them to our foundation for information, and, I hope, save a life.

When I'm on stage making my corporate presentations, people in the audience can easily see the hot pink polish. I can read their faces as they sit and look curiously at my pink finger waving around as I speak. As I begin to talk about emotional branding I point out that people do not respond to policy and procedure and features and benefits— they respond to something that is meaningful, personal, relevant, and emotional.

At this point I stop and say, "Raise your hands if you noticed this."

I put my hand out for all to see my pinky. Almost everyone in the audience raises their hands. I say, "Good, I'm going to demonstrate how emotion and relevance to your life trumps policies, procedures, features, and benefits. I'm going to present the same information to you twice. You decide which presentation generates interest. Here's the first: I am involved in an organization that teaches child safety in and around the home. Our foundation has a Web site and hands out brochures and furniture safety straps at meetings and trade shows. We speak at parent groups and day care council meetings. We are educating parents and caretakers and spreading the word on child safety. Now, based on that presentation, how inclined would you be to want to get involved? Please raise your hands if this sounds intriguing to you."

Of course, no one raises a hand. Then I say, "Of course not. There are hundreds of organizations and foundations out there vying for your attention. Why would this particular one be any different, right? Now let me show you how I'm going to get your attention and get your interest. Remember, I'm doing this to demonstrate the power of emotion and the importance of relating to another person's values. Here is the second presentation: Please raise your hands if you have children or grandchildren."

The majority of the audience always raises their hand. "Good. Now, I want you all to close your eyes. I want you to picture your child or your grandchild. Now, please recall what it feels like when you're with that child: if the child is small, how you feel holding him or her, tucking your baby into bed, giving your baby a bath. If the child is older, imagine how you feel just spending time with him or her—laughing, hugging, telling that child of yours how much you love them. Feel it!

Good. Now, I want you to imagine you just got a phone call, and you will never see that child again. Please open your eyes. That's the call I got." And I go on to tell how I heard what happened to Amaya, ending with, "She was one month shy of turning three."

The entire room lets out an audible gasp, and I can instantly see and feel the sympathy. Then I say, "Please, I don't want your sympathy. I don't need it. But I want to tell you that after my wife and I emerged from shock, we asked ourselves how this freakish, once-in-a-lifetime tragedy could happen to us. This has to be the freakiest of freak accidents!" But of course it's not. And I reel off the horrifying statistics and talk about what we do in our unrelenting mission to make sure this preventable disaster comes to an end.

"Now, based on that presentation, how many of you would be inclined to get involved in my foundation?" Every hand in the room goes up.

I don't give them the name of the foundation, because I'm not on stage to push my agenda. I'm hired by my client to teach their attendees how to better communicate, manage and grow their business, and prosper. This is merely one example of how to do just that.

I continue, "I'm telling you this for one very simple reason. Every person and every organization must have a core purpose. Along with that core purpose comes a set of core values. I know my purpose in life. It's two-fold. First, I am on a mission to help organizations and individuals create a meaningful, profitable, and sustainable professional life. Second, I am on a mission to save young children from preventable and horrific tip-over deaths. Once you know your purpose, and you believe in it with all your heart, you must surround yourself with people who believe in your purpose as well. Then you must communicate to your employees, friends, colleagues, customers, loved ones, and the media in a way that is laced with emotion, relevance, and intrigue. Every conversation, advertising message, and interaction must make people around you ask, 'What's up with that?' 'Why are you doing that?' 'Tell me more.' 'You're kidding!' 'Can I help?' 'Do you have any openings?' 'I want some; how can I get it?'"

After all that I pause, raise my hand, showing my pinky, and I say to my audience, "Here's my question to you: What's your purpose?"

INTRODUCTION

I have always had a strong sense of purpose in life, and I have tried to pursue it with the core values I have consciously lived for decades. What happened to my granddaughter and to our entire family served to crystallize my values, however, and to make my purpose bigger than it ever was. It has also inspired me to write this book, because I believe that today, more than ever, individuals and companies have the power to truly effect change, but too many of them are focused on policies and procedures instead of values and purpose. And without values and purpose, that power and ability to influence too often goes to waste or even becomes destructive.

There have been plenty of examples of that over the last decade or so, beginning with the Enron scandal, in which unethical business behavior brought down a huge corporation and ruined the lives of thousands of employees and investors. That was followed by the proliferation of shady banking and real estate practices that rocked not only the US economy but also that of the entire world; the lingering aftermath still negatively affects the lives of millions. Even more recently there have been revelations about General Motors and its automobile recall policy that bring into question its approach to profits versus public safety.

When I wrote my first book, *The Brand Who Cried Wolf*, I drew on a philosophy that I had long advocated in my presentations, keynote speeches, training programs, and consulting arrangements with major corporations, small businesses, and nonprofit groups around the world. I had developed that philosophy from my earliest days as an advertising and marketing professional, and it was based on a core value my parents taught me: respect for humanity. From that core value emerged related values about honesty and integrity. That core value also helped me to realize my purpose, which was to help people be successful in any endeavor by focusing on what matters most to them and what matters most to those they serve. That is how the trajectory of my career moved in the direction of public speaking, where I could connect simultaneously with hundreds and sometimes thousands of individuals. To this day, nothing gets me more amped up than to engage a room or an auditorium full of people and show them the process for business success.

One of the reasons I love business—why I love what it stands for—is that it is a way for people to express their values. I love that someone can have an idea and use passion, smarts, and hard work to make a go of it. I've run my own business, served on boards, and started an international organization with three other partners. Over the course of my career, I've helped take three companies to IPOs. The reason I've been part of these things is because I believe in business, commerce, and capitalism. And I believe I have the right formula not only for helping new businesses get off the ground, but also for helping people create lasting, meaningful organizations.

Capitalism Is Not a Value-Neutral Machine

Throughout this book I argue that all sustainable businesses are built on a set of carefully developed and specific values that are woven into the very fabric of the organization's daily work. It may seem that there are companies that become so big they can lose their way in terms of values that guide planning and decision making, and still, despite this loss of direction, not fail. These are companies that have hundreds of millions in liquid assets. This, however, is just an illusion. Because success is not measured solely in financial profit.

Wait! Don't tell me. I can hear it now: the cries of outrage across the business landscape that I am promoting an anti-capitalist idea. "What about profits! What about the free market!" That's just hysteria based on ignorance of what the concept of capitalism really means. It is a complete misconception that capitalism is a single-minded, moneymaking machine. Capitalism is not a machine! It is a directed or purpose-driven system of economic exchange that human beings have created—human beings who have values!

Think about it this way. If you ask the average guy or gal on the street whether or not they think killing someone exclusively and expressly in order to make a profit is permissible, they'd probably say no. That means that these people do not believe that financial profit is the exclusive instrument by which success is measured. So why do we make the mistake of conceiving of business as a merely profit-directed enterprise?

There is no doubt that financial profit is a significant goal of any business venture. Breaking even is not the dream. And in a sense, failure means going out of business, so that's not the dream, either. No one in business wants to fail, and no one goes into business expecting to do that. But failure happens on a daily basis all around the world. Sometimes, it's truly out of our control, such as when natural disasters occur. But what about the failure that takes place because you didn't create a relevant personal purpose to guide you in making solid decisions and creating a culture of meaning in your organization? Then the failure is on you.

Starting your own business, managing a business, and running or being part of a team is exciting. Although much of the focus in this book is on creating success in business based on clearly articulated values and purpose, the fact is that there is no real distinction between the values that drive successful businesses to realize their purpose and the values that drive other parts of our lives.

Most of us don't want to be a person with one set of values at work and a different set in our private lives, although we sometimes feel pressured to segment ourselves instead of remaining as integrated wholes. The result is a kind of silo effect that separates people from each other in terms of the roles they play at work and at home. It's not surprising that we have created these artificial boundaries, given how many advances occurred in the twentieth century at such an astonishing rate of speed. The world simply changed too fast for us to keep up. A coping mechanism—or, if you prefer, a strategy for making sense of what was happening—was to conceptually box everything up: to compartmentalize, categorize, and separate.

Moreover, people didn't always know how to apply their values in this rapidly changing environment. In the business world, there was the complicating factor of amnesia: too many people had somehow forgotten that capitalism is not equivalent to greed. Sure, people have been greedy since, well, people have existed. That's no surprise, but it's also not the only way we're hardwired to be. Humans have a tremendous capacity for empathy—which I'll discuss later—that isn't exactly conducive to greediness.

Nevertheless, I also believe that greed is a value. Gordon Gekko definitely thought it was! The question I have for you in this book is whether or not it's your value. If it is, how does it contribute to and guide your purpose? I submit to you that greed—brute selfishness—is not a value worthy of anyone who respects humanity.

Because my area of expertise is business, I spend a lot of time thinking and talking about all types of organizations, from the non-profit to the international conglomerate. But this book is for anyone who wants to do and be better. It's for anyone who wants to engage thoughtfully with what it means to identify one's values and purpose, create a culture around those values and purpose, use them to guide decision-making, connect with those who share them, and generate a profitable, sustainably successful personal and professional life.

It is aimed at individual leaders—whether they're in a position of leadership or not. You may be a manager who wants to move up, a supervisor who wants to connect with those under your responsibility, or a CEO who needs to set a new course for a company. You may want to lead a sales department, a group of tourists through a museum, or a cause you believe is more important than your own status in life. You may be a natural-born leader and haven't realized it yet. Or you may be someone who has the passion and knowledge to accomplish great things—but who never thinks in terms of leadership. Whatever your situation, you're going to find the tools to help you lead and succeed through clearly articulated values and purpose.

This book focuses specifically on how you can identify your values and your purpose, and how you can build an organization, a team, or a cause around them. This is truly a book on how your values can lead to success.

Some chapters lean on conceptual knowledge, while others use case studies to help you develop the skills you'll need to create a values-based culture. In all cases, however, this book aims at being accessible and engaging.

Deciding to write this book and then working out the details of what I believe about the relationships among values, purpose, and a successful life has been a rewarding experience. I hope that you find the reading rewarding as well. After all, it's a good idea to pause and reflect on what you are doing with your life, what your values are, and how they influence the choices you make and the people around you. In the hustle and bustle of modern life, we may find ourselves pressed for time, but if we understand how important this practice of contemplation is, we can always find a quiet space to do it. As Socrates famously said, "The unexamined life is not worth living."

CHAPTER 1

DEFINE SUCCESS IN TERMS OF VALUES, THEN LEAD

Try not to become a man of success,
but rather try to become a man of value.
—Albert Einstein

In the business world, values—at least those unrelated to generating profits—haven't always had a fair hearing. And that's unfortunate, because the belief that any values unrelated to profits are irrelevant to business success is just wrong. Nevertheless, this belief has dominated our culture for decades and has redefined capitalism as a single-mindedly voracious moneymaking machine. Yet we all know that businesses are created and run by people.

People have values that form the foundation of their lives. It is these values that drive their decision-making and direct their goals. So why should we believe that business could be immune from values, especially when business is understood as a type of enterprise in which people interact? In fact, business is the perfect environment in which to live out our abiding values. Starting a new business is creative, empowering, and exhilarating. Most of all, it's an act of hope and belief in yourself and your ideas. But what, exactly, does that mean?

Believing in yourself is not an exercise in stroking your ego. Believing in your ideas is not about being uncritical or avoiding the sometimes-painful process of self-reflection. Instead, believing in yourself is about upholding your core values, the things that make your life meaningful. These values guide the decisions you make about what to do or not to do. We sometimes have a clear purpose in mind but are still unclear about the values that will help us realize it. In that case, the first step toward that goal is to identify those values and work toward understanding how they fit together.

On occasion that means stepping out of one's comfort zone.

When I was a young man, I was absolutely terrified of public speaking—I mean, utterly petrified! I just couldn't do it. Sure, I was perfectly at ease with my friends, who thought I was charming and funny. And maybe after a few beers I could also impress some strangers. But ask me to get in front of a room full of people and speak, and forget it! I'd break out in a cold sweat. It was so bad that my worst college memories were not of hangovers or a broken heart but of having to make presentations or give speeches in class.

By the time I started my own advertising agency, I realized I needed to do something about my phobia. I explicitly said, "The only way I'm going to be successful is to be a good public speaker. I need to learn how to do this." So I decided to practice, to face my fear head-on. I started by volunteering to speak at places like Rotary Club meetings and Chamber of Commerce events. These were generally small audiences; I didn't go from zero to sixty! Eventually, however, I got comfortable enough to realize that public speaking wasn't going to kill me. In fact, I realized that having the ability to connect with large groups in a formal setting and communicate an important message with passion and conviction was something of value in and of itself! And that has contributed greatly to a very successful life.

Obviously, overcoming your shortcomings or anxieties to realize a better version of yourself is significant. But sometimes the goal is much bigger: to make the world a better place. Just ask Malala Yousafzi, the young Pakistani girl whose desire to be educated was almost killed—literally—by the Taliban, who, in October 2012 shot her and some of her classmates in the head. Thrust into the spotlight, Malala did not shy away from leading the cause for education for girls across the world. In less than a year, she was addressing the United Nations, and not long after that, the teenager was nominated for the Nobel Peace Prize.

Now an education activist, Malala is more determined than ever to convince others that education is a right for all children, wherever they are. In her address to the United Nations on July 12, 2013—her sixteenth birthday—she said, "The terrorists thought that they would change my aims and stop my ambitions, but nothing changed in my life, except this: weakness, fear, and hopelessness died. Strength, power, and courage were born." All of us are inspired by someone so young who is so clear in her purpose and the values that support it.

Whoever you are and wherever you are, you can start taking steps to create lasting success in your personal and professional life by identifying your values and purpose. Too often, however, the process of articulating those things gets lost in the excitement and details of starting something new, such as a business venture, a volunteer group, or any other new enterprise. The following situation is a good example.

A Values-in-Action Case Study: The Hypothetical "Flower Power" Flower Shop

Suppose, for a moment, that your dream is to open a flower shop. You've got the training in floral arranging. Maybe you've got a degree in botany or a related field. You've worked up a business plan, found a terrific location, have a network of solid suppliers, and even have the business name, Flower Power. But you're not yet financially stable enough to bring on employees.

At this point in the process, it's easy to see that the entire business is you. You're doing it all: the books, the paperwork, the marketing, and working with customers and suppliers. Pretty much all the operational details are your responsibility. And because you have to learn all the ins and outs of your new business very quickly, you have a global view of what Flower Power is, how it works, and what can be done to grow the business.

Whether you realize it or not, you are your business's leader. You not only have knowledge of the mechanics of running it, you also have something more. If you're a reflective, thoughtful person, you understand what's important to making Flower Power a success: the knowledge of your values—the core beliefs about what is important to do and be.

Now suppose after a year or so you were able to bring on your first hire. This valued and trusted employee didn't have the experience at first to move into a management position, and anyway, the business wasn't ready to support that. At some point, however, that employee knew how to do the job inside and out and learned enough about management within the company to be considered for promotion. He or she had developed the skills. But what about the values behind Flower Power? Were these shared as well?

If Flower Power is going to grow into everything you dream it can be, you not only have to articulate your values, they have to be stated and lived in a way that permeates the entire business. They have to color every decision, from choosing the materials you use to hiring new employees or taking on certain clients.

Success ultimately comes down to one's ability to articulate values, create a framework or culture built around those values, and lead others to the mission or purpose.

So let's consider the first step: Can you identify your values?

CHAPTER 2

IDENTIFY YOUR VALUES

It is not in the still calm of life, or the repose of a
pacific station, that great characters are formed.
The habits of a vigorous mind are formed in
contending with difficulties. Great necessities call
out great virtues . . . qualities which would otherwise
lay dormant wake into life and form the character of
the hero and the statesman.
—Abigail Adams

The dictionary defines *value* as a principle or quality that is valuable or desirable. I can't say that is a particularly helpful definition, but it does describe the quandary that many of us face when we try to articulate our values.

It may be that you need to point to some example. It's sort of like the famous quip from Supreme Court Justice Potter Stewart: "I can't define it, but I know it when I see it."[1] The "it" he was referring to was pornography, but, really, there are many things we can't define formally but seem to be able to identify in action with no trouble. That's odd, isn't it? Yes and no. It's strange, but it's also rather common.

For example, you might not be able to define "good," as in morally good, but you may be successful at consistently identifying those actions you call good. This is a difficulty facing most of us who try to define values, among other things. I was in a café in Rome when a couple sat down next to me. I overheard them talking and pegged them as American. As it happened, they were from somewhere around Chicago. We started chatting, and since we were all navigating our way in a foreign country, the conversation turned to language.

"It's the strangest thing," the husband said with a laugh. "I met someone in a store and was trying to explain 'cheesy.' It took me something like five or six times—and not because the guy didn't speak some English or I didn't speak some Italian. We were able to communicate fairly well. The problem," he continued, "was that I had trouble defining it. I know cheesy when I see it and hear it, but for the life of me, I couldn't explain it!"

This happens sometimes with concepts that imply some kind of critical assessment, like *cheesy*, and it frequently occurs with more subtle and abstract terms. For example, I could define "value" as a guiding principle of action. But a "guiding principle of action" generally means morally correct attitudes or behaviors. So, the definition of *value* as a morally correct attitude or behavior doesn't really get us very far. After all, what does "morally correct attitude or behavior" mean? As we will see, there are quite a few ways in which we can answer that question, and each answer is mainly an intellectual framework within which to understand existing beliefs.

So, let's go back to some examples. Notice the way each question is answered, and consider whether or not you think the answer defines one of your values:

1. If you make a mistake that you know has or will yield a negative result for your employer, do you tell your supervisor or someone at work?
    a. Yes. I am the sort of person who does not like negative consequences.
    b. Yes. I am the sort of person who believes I must be honest in my interactions.
    c. No. I am the sort of person who protects my own self-interests.

2. Have you ever taken office supplies home with you for your personal use?
    a. Yes. I am the sort of person who believes it's okay to take a little from work because I give back in many ways.
    b. No. I am the sort of person who does not take what is not mine.

3. If your supervisor treats a subordinate poorly, what would you do?
    a. I would not say anything because I am the sort of person who believes it's not a good idea to get involved in the business of others.
    b. I would say something because I am the sort of person who believes no one should treat others poorly.

4. If you see or hear an employee undermining a supervisor's directions, what would you do?
   a. I would not say anything, because I am the sort of person who believes it's not a good idea to get involved in the business of others.
   b. I would say something because I am the sort of person who believes that undermining the chain of command leads to problems.

5. Have you ever felt as if your employer didn't value your contributions?
   a. Yes. I am the sort of person who wants to be acknowledged for what I contribute.
   b. No. I am not the sort of person who needs to be acknowledged for what I contribute.

6. If you're late for work, are you honest about why you're late?
   a. Sometimes, so long as it's a good reason. I am the sort of person who doesn't like to look bad.
   b. Yes. I am the sort of person who believes that being honest in all my interactions is good.
   c. Never. I am the sort of person who doesn't like to look bad. I'll say whatever is necessary to make my reason acceptable.

The important thing to focus on here is whether or not you believe the reason or reasons given are good ones, because that is often very helpful to the process of defining your values apart from some context. Moreover, the process of defining values helps you get a clearer idea about the sort of person you want to have in your business, whether they are employees, colleagues, suppliers, or clients. All this is part of defining values.

So far I haven't been very explicit about the values I think are important; I wanted to concentrate on how you identify your values and your purpose. But I do think there are some basics that are essential for anyone's success. First is respect for other human beings. All people are equally valuable. Second is honesty. Deceiving others may seem like a short-term solution to a problem, but it ultimately harms both you and the person you deceive. If nothing else, deception steals choice. If I deceive you, I am essentially preventing you from making a choice; in my deception, I'm making your choice for you. These are my values and I know without a shadow of a doubt where they come from.

"Know Thyself"

The saying that forms the title of this section was inscribed above the entrance to the ancient temple of Apollo at Delphi, in Greece. I believe this states one of the most important principles for understanding your values.

Bar none, my father was the greatest gentleman on the planet. He instilled in me respect for others—especially women—in ways that showed how ahead of his time he was. "If I ever find out you treated a woman as less than a woman, you'll have me to answer to," he often admonished my brothers and me, in his steady and clear voice. From the time we were little, he expected us to adhere to certain values that he believed were timeless, even if others hadn't yet caught on.

His belief about treating women well wasn't a macho thing; it was about equality, fairness, and respect. My father lived in an era when women had to fight for their place in business, and they were often

treated disparagingly. In my area of expertise, advertising and marketing, sexual harassment was par for the course well into the 1980s. (If
you've ever seen the television show *Mad Men,* you know what I'm
talking about.) So, by the time I had become an adult and started my
own business, I had internalized the lessons my father taught me.

For example, my agency had a distributor client in the Southeast
who supplied products to several hundred independent contractors
throughout the region. When we ran advertising programs for the distributor, we were essentially creating and managing the advertising for
all of the distributor's contractors. During a specific campaign, one of
his contractors felt the need to contact our office on a regular basis.
This guy had always been rather abrasive and bombastic, but one day
he crossed the line. He was remarkably abusive to one of my employees, who happened to be a woman. She came to me extremely upset
and said she was unwilling to work with him and was concerned about
how the client would respond and how her decision would impact my
relationship with my client.

"Doesn't matter," I told her. "No one treats people at this company
the way this guy treated you and gets away with it."

"I don't know, Scott. Are you sure?" She was well aware that this
distributor account was worth almost half a million dollars per year.

"If we lose 'em, we lose 'em," I told her. I wanted her and everyone in my agency to know that I valued them as people, not just as
employees, or worse yet—as the client's servants.

The next thing I did was to get on the phone with this particular
contractor.

"We've got a problem," I told him. "You crossed the line. You're
abusive and offensive. You're out of the campaign."

He didn't believe me at first. Instead, he joked a bit. Then when he realized I was not kidding around, he started pleading, trying his best to get me to change my decision. I would not.

The next thing I knew, my distributor client, Roger, called me.

"Scott, what's going on? I just got a call from one of my guys. He says you cut him off at the knees."

I told him the story, and, like his contractor, he tried to make light of it. Finally, I said, "Listen, Roger, if you need to drop my agency in order to save face with your customer, then do so, but I'm not going to allow anyone to treat my people badly."

In the end, the contractor was cut from the campaign, and we held onto the distributor account. Eventually, Roger applauded my decision, telling me he respected what I did and would have done the same thing. None of this would have happened, though, if I hadn't known myself well enough to know what I stand for. In other words, I know my values. And I value treating people with decency more than I value a buck—in business as in life.

Come On! Is There Really Any Such Thing as "Business Values"?

A simple Internet search using the key words "business values" will get you an amazing array of hits. Some involve financial values—things like low-cost goods and services—but most involve corporate or company values. This reflects an increasing trend in current thinking about business values to tie together the individual and the value, and collections of individuals around values.[2]

A 2011 USA Today column by Steve Strauss focuses on the crucial connection between individual and business values. "Businesses are run by people," he writes, "people have values that are important to them, and those values are reflected in those businesses."[3] Strauss finds it easiest to see the connection in smaller businesses, like TOMS Shoes. TOMS adopted a practice of giving away one pair of shoes to a needy child for each pair purchased. That resonated with customers, and the company took off.

Big companies can also live out the values of their founders. Strauss points to Starbucks, which purchases health insurance for employees who work for the company a minimum of twenty hours per week. That's because, as a child, founder Howard Schultz and his family were deeply impacted by a lack of health insurance.

Strauss is correct when he claims, "If making a buck is your bottom line, you will make different choices than, say, if building a brand or creating mutual value is your priority." Wherever your values inform your decision-making processes, so, too, will they inform the sorts of choices you make. And that, in turn, colors the experience your customers have every time they step into your store, navigate to your Web site, or call your company. That experience is part and parcel of the culture of your business.

Culture is another thing that can be difficult to define. In its most comprehensive terms, culture is a set of practices and institutions that reflect the group's beliefs—such as religion and morality—as well as their artistic, intellectual, and technological accomplishments. For a business, culture is typically discussed in directional terms: It can be "bottom-up" or "top-down." A bottom-up approach to an organization's culture means that those whose boots are on the ground are setting the tone for how things are done, both substantively and stylistically, within parameters provided from above. A top-down approach, on the other hand, involves an organization's leaders setting standards for everything from office conduct to office décor. The reality for most enterprises is probably somewhere in the middle. After all, culture is developmental and fluid.

This is not to say culture is as fickle as this year's fashions, but with myriad personalities involved in a business's daily operations, there are bound to be adjustments. At the core of the culture, however, are values that do not change. Values dictate what people do and also often how they decide to do what they do. In other words, values involve ethical decision-making.

A Case Study in Defining Values: My Ad Agency

Many years ago, I was working with a large utility company headquartered in southern New York. We had just been hired to create and run several promotions. My client contact—a woman I initially thought was wonderful and very bright—was the marketing director. The first time I met her in my offices, she exuded confidence, knowledge, and creativity. I loved working with her.

Not long after we had begun working together, we scheduled a meeting at the client's headquarters. I was to meet with her and her boss, the vice president. We had agreed on a date and a very specific time. Now the one thing I have always been, if anything, is practically neurotic about being early to every meeting and every event. So I drove to my meeting and arrived twenty minutes early.

No sooner had I walked in the door than the marketing director came out and exclaimed, "You're late! You were supposed to be here forty-five minutes ago!"

"Hang on," I responded, feeling a bit flummoxed. I took out my calendar and showed her the time I had written down while she was in my office at our initial meeting. I also reminded her of the call I had made to her two days earlier to confirm the meeting time.

"Well," she said, "just tell Brian your car broke down."

"What?" I asked her, incredulous. "I can't tell him that. Why don't I just tell him I got the time mixed up?"

"No!" she responded emphatically. "You can't tell him that, because I'm responsible for setting the meeting times. Just tell him your car broke down."

So we went into the meeting with her boss, Brian, and I began to apologize for being late, even though I knew I wasn't. I then proceeded to tell this story of how my car broke down.

Things went downhill from there. He then started asking what happened. I couldn't think how to respond, because I'm not good with cars, so I said, "The fan belt snapped." It was all I could come up with.

"No problem. We have some guys here who can look at your car to make sure you're okay heading back."

"Thanks, that's really generous, but no. I'm all set. I'm good with cars."

At this point, I just wanted to crawl under a rock. This was one of the most uncomfortable situations I have ever been in. First, I had to ad lib a lie to a brand-new client whom I had just met. Second, I now knew my contact at this company was the type of person who looked out only for herself, no matter what. She valued her own image more than the truth. She would not admit she made a mistake with the time, even if it meant compromising another person.

As our business relationship grew, there were more and more instances of her saying things like, "I never told you that," when she had, or "Why didn't you ship that out?" when she had told me to hold off. The situation became very difficult, and eventually, we mutually decided it was best to part ways. We clearly had very different values.

Now, for just a minute, I want you to consider your values. Think, for example, about the way you treat your kids, your employees, your grocer, or your dry cleaner. Why do you treat them the way you do? Now remember some of your recent decisions—in business or in daily life. What were they? How did they reflect your values? Did anyone disagree with your decision because his values were fundamentally different from yours? Or did anyone agree with your decision because her values were fundamentally in line with yours?

The source of our values is the topic of the next chapter, to which we will turn once you've had some time to reflect on these questions.

CHAPTER 3

DETERMINE THE SOURCE OF YOUR VALUES

THE POINT WHICH I SHOULD FIRST WISH TO UNDERSTAND

IS WHETHER THE PIOUS OR HOLY IS BELOVED BY

THE GODS BECAUSE IT IS HOLY, OR HOLY BECAUSE

IT IS BELOVED BY THE GODS.

—PLATO

The fact is, not everyone shares the same values. And even when they do, they don't always come to those values the same way. Some people will tell you they get their values from their religious tradition. Others will say their values are derived from their family, from the way they were raised. Still others will tell you personal experiences taught them about what's important. Each of these is not only an explanation of one's values but also a justification for one's actions. It's important to understand this distinction for reasons that will become clear as we discover our purpose, surround ourselves with those who share that purpose, and work to promote it.

To make each of these ideas clear—explanation and justification—consider the following scenario:

The Origin of Values: A Hypothetical Situation

Person X runs a medium-size investment firm with comfortable offices for his dozen or so employees and a nice conference room that is in frequent use for meetings with prospective clients. This is not the only investment firm in town. Competition is lively from several other enterprises. Early one winter morning, an accidental electrical fire breaks out in the offices of one of those competitors. Later that day, after hearing the news, Person X calls a meeting with his senior management team and tells them he would like to offer the use of their offices to this competitor until they get back on their feet. One manager is concerned that they will learn their process and steal their client list. Another manager says "They're competition. Let them figure out how to deal with the fire." Yet another manager is concerned they will develop relationships with their top sales people and hire them away. Finally, another manager wants to know Person X's intentions. He believes Person X has an ulterior motive. After considering their input, however, Person X calls the other firm's head and offers to let that company use the conference room, computers, and other logistical resources. Then Person X spends the rest of the day rescheduling meetings and shuffling his staff around. Although valid concerns were raised by management, Person X decided to help anyway. Why did Person X do that?

Here are some possible explanations:

- The topic of Person X's religious service last week was beneficence—helping those in need.

- Person X believes he is obligated to help people whenever he can.

- Person X is the sort of person who innately, almost without thinking about it, helps out whenever he can.

- Person X believes that it's good for society when citizens help each other.

- Person X says that it just seemed like the right thing to do; pretty much everyone he knows would do the same thing.

Now, what would you have done, and, just as importantly, why? The example of helping someone in need is not particularly controversial, although the extent of the aid rendered may not seem very realistic.[1]

My point here is that despite the fact that the action is the same, the explanations for why Person X decided to help differ. They reflect a variety of common ethical theories: divine command theory, which reflects religious belief; duty-based ethics, which focuses on what we ought or ought not to do; virtue ethics, which is concerned with maintaining good character; utilitarian ethics, which looks at the greatest good for the greatest number; and relativism, which takes into account differences in culture, biology, and historical era, among other things.

It is not important that we delve deeply into these theories here. What is important is that you understand that your values have theoretical explanations that can help you clarify your own thinking about them. Not only do you need to be clear about what your core values are, you need to work out why these are your values. In other words, you need to grasp what it is about these values that make them meaningful to you. Having a theoretical understanding of your values is a part of what makes their meaning more robust. And this understanding will ultimately contribute to your leading the most successful life possible.

Justifying Values—Questions of Relativism

In a world where we interact with others across the globe either in person, by phone, or virtually, questions of relative values seem to arise more and more frequently. A certain type of relativist will say that the beliefs and practices of other cultures have their own internal coherence, and that you and I are not in any privileged position to evaluate those beliefs and practices, positively or negatively.

Imagine for a moment that you are doing business in Japan. If you accept a business card from a Japanese acquaintance or colleague and bend it or put it in your pocket, that person will be offended.[2] Does that seem odd to you? If so, why? If not, why not? Where does your response come from? Can you respect it or dig deep enough into the culture to understand it? In other words, can you explain it?

Now let's look at another scenario that is obviously more controversial. The reason for doing so is to introduce an important component of thinking about values—justification. When we assert a value, we should be able not only to explain it but also to justify it. Let's briefly return to the case of the aid rendered to the competing company. Someone may take issue with the rightness of having given that aid; another person may question why it was done. I hope this next scenario helps to clarify those two parts of our discussion of values:

Justifying Values: A Hypothetical
Case Study Based on Actual Events

A man finds himself in debt. One of his seven children needed surgery, and he had to borrow the money to pay for it. The arrangement he made was to pay back the debt within a year. Like most of us, this man considers repayment of debt a value; the manner in which it is repaid is also a value. As the due date for repayment draws closer and he realizes he will not be able to meet it, the man decides to strike another bargain with the lender.

Here is where the man's story undoubtedly diverges from our own experience: In exchange for payment of the debt, he agrees to turn over his eight-year-old daughter to the lender's family so she can be married to the lender's teenage son.[3] The man has consulted with the elders in his community, and they have advised him that tradition dictates he turn over his daughter or repay the debt.

This situation is so far from most of our daily lives that it seems like fiction. In fact, you might find it so completely at odds with your own worldview that you can't relate to it at all. This is not a bad thing! In fact, it's part of the reason I'm including it. If you find yourself saying, "Well, what's this got to do with me? I'd never be in that sort of situation," you need to ask yourself why it doesn't apply to you. With that question, you are beginning to wrestle with what your values are and how they differ from those that govern this man's life.

This story has a basis in fact, however, so how do we respond? Are we outraged? If so, who are we angry at and why? Do we accept the transaction as part of another's culture, even if we wouldn't condone it in our own?

Let me suggest a more familiar situation that we might also find difficult to accept as a value. Suppose, for example, that you are an attorney who is ethically and legally bound by attorney-client privilege. Now suppose you learn something about your client that you find despicable but that, because of that privilege, you cannot divulge to the court. Many people might say they would not become an attorney for precisely that reason, that their values would not allow them to remain silent in the face of some terrible truth. Others say the attorney is bound by his oath.

In the debt case study, the man's community promotes—and therefore justifies—the sort of practice described above. A relativist will accept that justification. Clearly, however, not everyone would agree with that view. We have only to look at human rights groups that argue it is never permissible to traffic human beings. A religious group might claim that God would not condone such a practice, while someone else could argue that using one's child to pay off a debt produces more good for society (or at least the family of the child) than not turning her over.

Notice that in addition to the value expressed and the explanation, there's also a justification of the value—a reason offered for a claim. We offer justifications when we want to convince someone (sometimes even ourselves!) that something is true or good.

Here's an example from a conversation my daughter Nicole had with a college classmate a few months ago; her justifications are italicized, while the result—the conclusion—is in bold type:

1. *My parents instilled in me the idea that stealing is wrong.*

2. *My parents instilled in me the idea that paying someone for what they've worked for and what they're selling is important.*

3. *Stealing from others has negative consequences to others, as well as to myself.*
   a. *These negative consequences are typically hurtful to myself and especially to others.*
   b. *These hurtful negative consequences are often difficult to overcome.*

For example, many recording artists are losing great sums of money because of illegal downloads.

4. Doing what results in hurt for myself or for others is wrong.

5. Therefore, stealing is wrong.

Notice that this reasoning involves piling up a series of reasons to believe that stealing is wrong. In our daily lives, this sort of formal justification process doesn't happen. Instead, it looks more like this exchange:

> Nicole: Why are you downloading that music for free? That's stealing. You should buy it from iTunes.
>
> Friend: What do you mean? Everyone does it! Why should I buy this stuff when I can get it for free?
>
> Nicole: What? Why should you buy that shirt then, if you can take it from a store and wear it for free?
>
> Friend: That's not the same thing. What's your problem with free downloads, anyway?
>
> Nicole: It's just wrong. Musicians make their living by selling their music, not by you getting it for free.
>
> Friend: What, are you, a musician? How would you know what they go through?
>
> Nicole: My dad wrote a book, and he has an audio book and other DVD products. If someone figured out a way to take my dad's stuff without paying

for it, he would lose a lot of money. I'm in college because my parents make a living.

Friend: I'm sorry. I see what you mean.

As you can see from this simple exchange, we spend a lot of time justifying our values, whether they're for the good or not. One of the ways we can effectively understand our values and provide solid justifications for them is to first think carefully about the theories that help us explain our values. Focusing on the process of justifying values happens to be an important component of creating a flourishing culture, as we'll see in a later chapter.

In the meantime, it's useful to recognize that sometimes our explanation and justification of values collapse into each other. You may find that you share values with someone who explains them differently from you or who justifies them differently. You may also find that you thought you shared values with someone until you have an occasion to have a values-oriented conversation with them. That has happened to me.

While I was running my agency, one of our clients cut their budget, and we had to temporarily lay off a few people. When they ramped back up, we brought our employees back, at least most of them. There was one young lady who, when we called her, said she would like to meet with my executive vice president and me.

After we assembled in my office, she said, "I have another offer for more money. Are you willing to match the offer?"

My vice president and I looked at each other, and we knew in our hearts that she was making this up. I could tell by the way she said it and the expression on her face that she was just lobbying for more money. I told her she should take the other offer; we weren't going to be able to match it.

She left, and I expected that she'd call a few days later to say that the other job had fallen through and she wanted to return. Instead, a few weeks after that we received notice from the unemployment office that she had filed for continued benefits, proof that she didn't have another offer. Why would she file for unemployment if she had another job lined up? My CFO came to me straight away.

"Scott, this was just wrong. She had an offer from us, and she refused it. Now she wants unemployment benefits."

I told him to let the unemployment office know the situation. He did, and she lost her benefits. Shortly thereafter, she called all her friends—former coworkers at my office—to let them know what happened.

Not long after that I was traveling with one of my account directors to a client meeting. She let me know what she thought about our treatment of the young woman, namely that what I did was wrong.

"Here are the facts," I said, explaining that we had offered her a job that she refused, but that she still attempted to collect unemployment benefits. "Look," I went on, "It's illegal and unethical for her to do such a thing."

"I disagree," she retorted. "You should have let her collect and not 'butt in' on her personal life."

"There's nothing about what she did that is relevant to her personal life." But just as quickly as I uttered those words, I knew that no matter how talented and charming this particular account director was, she was not healthy for my business environment. It was at that moment I discovered we had completely different values.

As you build your business, one of the important considerations is whether or not you think the values you share with your employees and colleagues should be explained and justified the same way.

Consider the ways the scenario involving the payment of debt was evaluated. Do you think the justification of one's values is as important as the values themselves? If so, why? If not, why not? Consider writing out an argument for one of your values.

Of course, knowing your values and where they come from is only a first step. It's time to consider the purpose you're going to use them for.

CHAPTER 4

HOW I UNCOVERED MY PURPOSE

THE BEST WAY TO NOT FEEL HOPELESS IS TO GET UP AND
DO SOMETHING. DON'T WAIT FOR GOOD THINGS TO HAPPEN
TO YOU. IF YOU GO OUT AND MAKE SOME GOOD THINGS
HAPPEN, YOU WILL FILL THE WORLD WITH HOPE, YOU
WILL FILL YOURSELF WITH HOPE.
—BARACK OBAMA

Values drive our lives toward the purpose we set for ourselves. They motivate us to do or not do certain things. When we lose sight of those values, in one way or another our lives fall apart. Purpose is the why something is done, the what-it's-for. This can be seen in terms of function. For example, the purpose of a knife is to cut. This can also be seen in terms of goal, or end. In that sense, the purpose of an acorn is to become an oak tree. To create a business based on values and meaningful purpose, then, is to provide a reason for its existence: a reason that makes sense to you, likely in terms of both function and goal.

I remember meeting a surgeon on a plane. We began chatting, and, like everyone else, his eyes kept dropping to my nail-polished finger. Finally, he saw me notice his stare. "So, what's that about?" he asked.

I told him Amaya's story and how my wife and I had decided we were going to respond to it. "We had to find purpose in the pain," I said.

He applauded our decision. "A knife can either serve you or hurt you," he said. "It just depends on which end you grab."

Your values guide you in the direction of your purpose. It's something like a marathon: You've got your finish line—that's your purpose. You need that finish line so you know where you're supposed to go. You also have a starting point and a map of the race's route. Those are your values. They help you get started; they guide you as you work toward your goal. They also collectively constitute that goal.

Remember, you're the one with the purpose, your purpose. You're the one with the values, your values. If you do not choose them, they're not yours. And when you do choose them, you obligate yourself to living up to them.

But what if you don't see how your values are going to lead to your purpose? And what if there are external pressures that can throw you off your pace? To continue the marathon analogy, maybe the weather the day of the race wears you down. Or maybe you get stuck in a pack of runners and have trouble breaking free. Obviously, the world would be much easier to navigate if our values were always supported by events around us or if there were a clear and untroubled connection between our purpose and our values. That's not always true, but you can help yourself a great deal by understanding how your values help you achieve your purpose.

Here's a personal story that will give you a better idea how I got to where I am today. I'm not telling this as an excuse to talk about the life and times of Scott Deming! I'm doing it to help you see the connection between values and finding your purpose. The experiences were so powerful that my response was visceral, and they molded me into the person I am today. As you read my story, think about what experiences have shaped you.

My degrees are in advertising and marketing. I discovered early on in college that the advertising and graphic design fields aligned perfectly with my creative bent. Once out of school, I began the search for the "perfect" job. A few years into the workforce, I landed an art director position at a small advertising agency in Houston, Texas. My direct supervisor was also the owner of the agency. His name was Paul, and he was one of the fairest, kindest, and most creative people I've ever known.

Even though I was only in my mid-twenties and still pretty wet behind the ears, Paul treated me with a great deal of respect. He trusted my creative direction enough to turn over some of his major clients to me. He would question and critique my work but never demean it. Before he sent me to client meetings, he'd say, "I have faith in you. You're a bright guy. I trust you better than I trust myself with this client." If something went wrong, he wouldn't yell or criticize; instead he would explain and teach. I never heard him talk about money, profit, margins, or billing. I only heard him talk about people and purpose.

Paul's mentoring instilled confidence in me, which in turn gave me a real sense of belonging, of being part of something special. When Paul and his partner left for a few days on a business trip, I still worked late, while many others skipped out for an early happy hour celebration. I felt I owed Paul and his company more than that.

Eventually, it was time to move on, and I left what turned out to be my favorite place to work, ever. I didn't realize until much later in my career just how special it was and what it meant to me or why I felt such a sense of loyalty, respect, and admiration for Paul.

My family and I moved to Ithaca, New York, where I landed a job as creative director for another small agency. Although I pretty much ran everything having to do with creative content and client contact for this agency and my boss gave me plenty of latitude for decision-making, the job lasted only one year. The reason? My boss, who also owned the company, was one of the worst human beings on the planet. Priority One in this guy's life was making a profit. And that was because his ultimate goal was not to work. All he cared about was getting through the week, getting out of the office as fast as possible on Friday afternoon, and not thinking about work again until he absolutely had to. His wife once told me that every Sunday evening he turned into a major ogre because he had to start thinking about the work week again.

The boss treated everyone in the organization like a beast of burden. He screamed, he shouted, he barked orders, and he never said, "please" or "thank you." He cut corners whenever possible if it made him money. He had no understanding of concepts like trust and loyalty. If you suggested that going above and beyond for a client was a good idea, he'd just stare at you like a horn had just sprung from your forehead, and then he'd start sputtering, his face beet-red, until he finally unleashed a torrent of expletives that, were they not so vile, would actually be impressive. His driving forces were money and selfishness.

Needless to say, he couldn't keep people around for very long. One day I finally quit on him. It wasn't that he'd done anything especially bad, it was just that I simply couldn't take it any longer. As I was walking out, he screamed, "I was going to turn this place over to you one day!"

"I don't need you or this place," I responded. "You can't kick people around like dogs and expect them to work for you. I'm starting my own agency, and I'll put you out of business!"

So, at the ripe old age of twenty-six, I started my own agency from the upstairs bedroom of our rented farmhouse. Within a year, I was leasing an office with two employees, and within a few more years I was employing eight people and doing a half-million dollars of business a year. Just a few years after that, I moved to Syracuse, New York, and grew the company into a multimillion-dollar national advertising agency.

Here's why I'm telling you all of this: Shortly after my departure from The Dictator in Ithaca, I began to reflect on my job with Paul in Houston. I realized that the reason I had worked so hard for him and felt such a sense of ownership and belonging is because Paul's values were in perfect alignment with mine and they matched our purpose, which was to provide the best work for our clients! Although I realize money is a necessity, it has never been a priority. Moreover, just like Paul, and in direct opposition to the other guy, my decisions, interactions, and conversations were guided by the values that also guided the other parts of my life. We didn't separate different aspects of our lives as The Dictator did. And when I worked hard for my clients— in the most fair and compassionate way possible, caring about their success as much as my own—and when I treated every employee like family, with the same level of care and concern I gave my own children, something amazing happened: I grew! And I kept growing!

When I decided to leave the agency business in 2004 and launch a speaking career, I did so for one reason: I knew that for me, advertising and marketing were only part of the success-and-happiness equation. I honestly felt there was something missing in the way people approached their work, careers, and businesses. In fact, because so many of my clients were expecting our advertising campaign to be a magic bullet and relied solely on advertising to drive their business, they didn't focus at all on the broader aspects of their company—their purpose or their culture. The longer I was in the ad business, the more apparent this became. At one point, while I was still running my own agency, we developed a division to train leaders, sales reps, and customer service reps within our clients' companies on how to communicate and collaborate internally and externally, to deliver expectations that went above and beyond. It was during this era of the agency, while we were training and helping our clients to hone their leadership, sales, and customer service skills that I decided, "This is where I want to be." And this is where I am!

Today, I work with those who want to improve, soar, and succeed. I speak, train, and consult with anyone who genuinely wants to take their career or their company to new heights. But the difference between where I am today compared to where I was many years ago is that I finally realized how important it was to seek out those whose values aligned with mine. Now, I work only with those people. I have walked away from contracts if it's obvious we do not agree on the basics of humanity or the concepts of what it takes to grow and sustain a business. If that seems harsh or counterintuitive to business and corporate life, I'll beg to differ all day long. When I decided to work with likeminded and like-spirited individuals and companies toward a common purpose, that's when my life changed for the better—forever.

My programs for improving personal and professional lives and creating personal and professional success and wealth—and my newest venture to transform home safety practices—are all infused by my values. As I've mentioned before, that's because I don't separate myself from my work. The guy you see at the grocery store, a backyard barbecue, or a national sales presentation is the same guy who started his own advertising and marketing business decades ago. Sure, the words I use when I speak to my wife are definitely not the same words I use when speaking before a crowd of 2,000, but I'm not referring to pillow talk! I'm referring to my character.

Since I was in my twenties, I have been talking about one essential value, and I grounded it in the psychological power of beliefs. "Our actions are based on the belief that what we do is good or will result in something good," I wrote in my book, *The Brand Who Cried Wolf*, at a time when many people felt like most large organizations were too large to care. From customer service to financial scandals, we were experiencing a crisis, and I wanted to call for something new. Well, not new exactly, but a return to values that authentically reflected the real meaning of business. Trust and loyalty were among them. As we all know, however, both trust and loyalty are hard to earn, easy to lose, and, once lost, almost impossible to regain. That's why I focused my purpose not just on businesses but also on individuals: on getting us back to our best selves, and, equally as important, on being individually responsible for what we say and do.

It's not always easy to sustain one's purpose. Even businesses that seem to clearly know what their purpose is sometime lose their way in a maze of bureaucracy.

Relevance, Meaning, and Personal Improvement
Trump Processes, Policies, and Procedures

What happens when a company and its employees seem to understand their values and care about their customers, but their workplace
policies and procedures prevent them from following through? Or
when an organization has policies and procedures in place, but the
people working there, from employees to senior management, simply
don't bother to uphold them?

Here's a perfect case in point. My wife and I have been customers of M&T Bank for many years. We do our personal banking there;
we do our commercial banking there; we have CDs and a savings
account with them, stocked with four years' worth of college tuition.
We helped our children open their own accounts there. Since my wife
goes through the local drive-through window many times per week,
she's on a first-name basis with most of the staff. Now, I know there
are much bigger, more important customers than us, but she's actually
treated like royalty when she goes inside!

Fifteen days after Amaya died, my wife walked into the branch to
open a checking account for the new foundation we started. All she
had was a letter from the IRS acknowledging that we were an entity.
After a lot of chatting about Amaya and an update on our kids, the
manager helped Deb open a retail account.

When our new foundation received its 501(c)(3) status, Deb
proudly went back to our local branch to do whatever she needed to
do now that we were officially tax exempt. The manager was confused,
however, as to what type of account we were supposed to have. She
called corporate, announcing her employee and branch number and

the fact that she was the branch manager; she noted that she was sitting with the customer and rattled off her reason for the call.

It happens that M&T has a policy where no employee is to pick up a call with a customer who has been transferred to them without knowing the reason for the call and the details of the situation. This is known as a "blind transfer," and we all know the "blind transfer" is ubiquitous in business, but M&T, valuing the customer experience, has decided (at least in theory) to eliminate this frustrating occurrence. They know how unproductive it is for the customer to repeat issues over and over again because nobody on the other end took the time to explain the situation while transferring the call. Apparently, however, either leadership did not effectively train the employees, or the employees simply did not care enough to follow procedure. Back to Deb.

After the branch manager explained the situation to someone at corporate, she was put on hold, then transferred. A new person at corporate picked up, and the branch manager had to repeat the information again. Once again she was transferred and put on hold. She was on hold for so long that she and Deb ran out of small talk. The situation was getting awkward. After waiting for far too long, the branch manager hung up and tried again . . . same details, account numbers, customer information, and reason for the call, and added that she was with the customer and the customer was getting a bit anxious. She was transferred, but this time to the wrong department. Though she tried to hide her exasperation, it was painfully obvious to her as a manager that she was experiencing exactly what her customers went through on a regular basis.

As a corporation, "customer delight" seems to be M&T's purpose. They apparently consider convenience and ease of doing business for their customers as a value—evident by the fact that they implemented the "no-blind-transfer" policy. However, it's painfully obvious to this customer—and my wife—that not every M&T employee has bought into that purpose. Where did M&T misstep? Why wasn't the corporate purpose relevant and meaningful to everyone within the corporation?

Tips for Making Values Relevant and Meaningful to One's Purpose

Here are some ways I've structured my thinking about using my values to work toward my purpose.

PROMISES

I try never to make promises I am not fully confident I can keep. No one can see the future, but as a general rule, we know pretty well what we can and cannot accomplish under the right conditions. I want to over-deliver, not under-deliver. I make sure to choose my commitments carefully so that I can successfully follow through.

PROFIT IS NOT THE BEST MEASURE OF MY SUCCESS

I don't get bogged down with sales quotas at the expense of my brand. Like everyone else, I have a business plan with goals and objectives. After all, in order to keep my business going and in order to make a living, I must make a profit. Profit is never my guiding force, however.

Remember, if money is your primary objective, your choices and interactions will be much different than if your primary objective is serving others and promoting success. But if you maintain a clear focus on your purpose, you're not going to have the time or inclination to worry about profit above all.

DIY

I avoid asking anyone in my organization to do anything I haven't tried myself. Of course, I may not have the requisite technical skill, but my point has more to do with making sure I am not being unreasonable in my expectations of others.

One of the best ways for you and everyone in your organization to gain appreciation for colleagues' expertise is to spend time in their shoes, or at least shadowing them. If you walk into someone's office and demand a specific assignment be completed by a certain dead-line—but you have no idea what goes into meeting that deadline— you're not only going to generate resentment from the people who are bending over backward to meet that deadline, but you're also not going to properly appreciate what's involved. On the other hand, if you know what you're asking people to do, you're likely going to help facilitate the work.

STAY HUMBLE

It's easy for me to find some new humbling experience. Wherever I go, I meet fascinating people who do exceptional things with their lives. That makes me reflect on my own life, and without fail, I am hum-bled. I'm not talking about some reaction for the moment but about changing your attitude—the way you approach your life every day. I realize that what's important to me is how I choose to conduct myself with others. Consider the details of another person's life, and you'll probably find something to appreciate. This type of story abounds! Just consider the following three stories:

It's How You Get in the Game: Winning

He made headlines: the kid from Rochester who loved basketball.[1] The kid with autism. The kid who was at every team practice and every game, handing out water and supporting the team he loved.

At the last game of the season, the coach told the kid to suit up. Toward the final minutes, the coach sent the kid in. After missing his first two shots, the kid made six three-pointers in a row. The last one was at the buzzer. The team won.

The entire gymnasium went crazy. Everyone descended onto the court to surround the new hero, the devoted kid whose coach and teammates loved him back.

Magic Moments: There Are No Secrets in the Face of Death

I've been a hobbyist magician since I was a kid. When I started volunteer work, I brought magic with me. It was always gratifying to bring a smile to the face of someone who was seriously or even terminally ill; to make them forget their situation for even a small moment.

One of my routine tours was the local cancer center's pediatric ward. It wasn't surprising to visit a child one week and find him gone the next. Gone—as in forever.

I will never forget one of those visits. A seventeen-year-old girl, ashen, her skeletal eyes ringed by dark circles, with a bandana covering her bald head, was too weak and irretrievably sad to smile.

I tried every trick I had, desperate to distract her from her plight. Finally, she responded with something resembling delight.

"How'd you do that?" she asked, wrinkling her brow.

"Oh, I'm sorry," I responded jovially. "I can't give away my secret."

Suddenly, her smile disappeared, and she just stared at me. "What does it matter?" she asked incredulously. "I'm going to be dead in two weeks."

I was stunned. For me to think about things like the magician's code when she was about to die changed everything in an instant.

Finally, I found my voice and apologized to her.

That was a humbling moment I'll never forget.

Worth the Wait: the Ultimate Customer Experience

There's a well-known story about a grocery store bag boy named Johnny who's worth the wait in line. In fact, he has such a following, that other checkout lanes sit empty while people queue up for Johnny. That's because he puts a note in their bag or gives them a hug when they leave. He simply makes people feel good, and he means it!

These stories remind me what it is to be humbled at the extraordinary feats of grace and courage and kindness that people can show each other. We should always search out these moments. We should always gain strength from these connections.

STAY CONNECTED

I never lose my personal connections. Technology is wonderful. E-mail, text messages, and the Internet are terrific tools, but they are not a substitute for personal contact. If your organization exists solely online, your challenge in pursuing your purpose is to create as much personal contact as possible by way of the user experience. If you do have face-to-face opportunities, make sure you don't let them go to waste!

Now let me ask you a question: How do you express your values in your personal and professional life? And how do you use them to uncover your purpose? The short answer is by using important critical thinking, as we'll see in the next two chapters.

CHAPTER 5

PURSUING YOUR PURPOSE THROUGH CRITICAL THINKING

THE MIND IS NOT A VESSEL TO BE FILLED,

BUT A FIRE TO BE KINDLED.

—*PLUTARCH*

Stephen Andras, head of family-owned Pioneer Basement Water-proofing in New England, had devoted himself and his company to a clearly articulated purpose and solid set of values from the very beginning.[1] For thirteen years he had a carefully worked out and continuous commitment to the highest customer service and water-proofing standards.

When he decided it was time to raise his company's $500,000 annual revenue, the real question was how to do it. He concluded he had to grow the business. After all, if he increased sales without a pro-portionate increase in personnel to support those sales, he wouldn't be able to provide the level of service that would guarantee results.

He decided to make the investment not just for the bottom line but also so that all his customers—existing and additional—could receive the excellent service that had solidified his reputation. Of course, growth was not without risk. It meant hiring twenty more employees—a 133 percent increase in personnel! But that investment paid off. With more workers came more work, and Andras's annual revenue rapidly increased to more than two million dollars a year. That was in 2006.

As recently as 2013, the Pioneer Basement Waterproofing Company was going stronger than ever. Developing and maintaining a solid reputation in an industry esteemed even lower than auto sales wasn't easy, but Andras held to familiar principles. "When a job goes wrong," Andras said in a 2006 interview, "you have to be able to face the problem and be up front and honest."[2] In addition, he vowed never to make a promise he could not live up to.

Let's consider these values for a moment. It may be difficult to "face up to problems and be honest," but it's not exactly an intellectual challenge. If you are committed to doing it and you know there aren't any exceptions to being honest, there's not a whole lot to figure out. But selective promise keeping is another matter altogether. How do you know when to make a promise and when not to do so? Answering that question is the result of considerable intellectual effort—what I'm going to call critical thinking.

Becoming a Critical Thinker

The topic of this book, as is clear by now, is how your values and purpose create meaning for your organization and lasting success for yourself. What we need to do now is spend time on an aspect of identifying and developing your values that will help you immensely in every facet of your life. That aspect is critical thinking.

You know how important it is to identify and develop your values. But just what is your purpose? And how do you know that your values will support it? Two words: critical thinking. You will need some serious critical thinking skills to home in on your purpose, to articulate it to others, and to plan how you will achieve it. Okay, but what is critical thinking?

"Critical" does not mean negative; we're not talking about telling someone what they've done wrong. The word can be traced back to Greek origins, and it's useful to follow this trail for a little bit. Related to the meaning of "critical" are verbs such as "separate," "discern," "distinguish," "pick out," "choose," "decide," "judge," "estimate," "bring to trial," and "accuse," and nouns such as "judgment," "standard," "criterion," and "tribunal." You can see a number of judicial associations with the term.

Less obvious, but just as significant, are medical associations that emphasize a crisis, turning point, or decisive moment. So thinking critically encompasses the urgency of crisis; the rule of a standard or criterion; the analytical processes of discerning, distinguishing, separating, and choosing; and the conclusiveness of judgment.

Most of us don't believe we need any training to be good critical thinkers. After all, we've been thinking and deciding all our lives. True enough. But how often have you taken a mental step back and asked yourself to reflect on that thinking? How often have you consciously observed your thinking, let alone your process of reasoning toward a decision? Probably far less frequently than you believe.

We are so intimately connected with our own thinking that it's easy to believe we are already really good thinkers. It's actually quite difficult to become an observer of your own thinking, since observing is a form of thinking! But there are techniques you and the people in your organization can use to support, develop, and hone your existing skills.

Support, Develop, and Hone Your Skills

During my training programs and seminars, I spend time discussing what I call "The Art of Communication." And a major component of this is understanding the importance of avoiding dangerous assumptions. To demonstrate this, I take the audience through an exercise.

First I have everyone stand, and then I ask the audience members to partner up. Once they've done this, I ask one of the partners to please pick up a pad and a pen or pencil. I then continue: "Now, I want the person holding the pad and pen to please turn around and face the back wall. I don't want you to see the screen, and you cannot turn back toward the screen until I give you permission to do so. I want the other partner to continue facing the screen.

"In a minute, I'm going to put a picture up on the screen. Please listen carefully to my instructions. I want the person facing the screen to help the person facing the wall to draw the picture."

At this point, everyone starts to laugh or moan, wondering how they're going to do this and do it correctly.

Then I say, "Do you all understand?"

Everyone says, "Yes," or "Yup," or "Let's do this."

I then put a very obscure picture on the screen, something literally impossible to describe. I give the group a minute to complete the exercise, then I scream, "Stop! Everyone turn around and see how you did."

People turn around, and the room gets loud with laughter and lighthearted discussions of the funny picture they came up with.

Then I say, "Okay, everyone please sit down. I want to ask you all a question, and I want you to be completely honest with me. Please raise your hands if you can answer yes to this question: How many of you facing the screen physically took the pen or pencil and began to draw for your partner?"

No one raises a hand.

Then I ask, "Why not?"

And the comments begin to flow: "You said we couldn't." "That would be cheating." "It would be against the rules."

This happens every time I do this exercise, whether there are thirty executives or five hundred sales reps.

After hearing their reasons, I say, "Please listen carefully to my instructions again. I said, 'I want the person facing the screen to help the person facing the wall to draw the picture.'"

Everyone typically begins to laugh and exclaim "Oh!" or "Ah-ha!"

I then say, "Every one of you highly intelligent adults made the wrong assumption. This was not an exercise to see how well you could describe a picture to another person. It was an exercise to show you the dangers of making assumptions. You all assumed that because I asked one person to pick up the pad and pen that the other partner could not touch it, correct?"

"Yes, correct," they respond.

"If you all made the wrong assumption just now," I go on, "based on some pretty straightforward instructions, can you imagine how many times during the course of each and every day you're making the wrong assumptions with colleagues, clients, and loved ones? The point of the exercise is to make you aware of assumptions you make and inferences you draw without really thinking about them. We're going to spend a lot of time thinking!"

SUPPORT

To support your purpose, you, and everyone in your organization, has to be willing to hear each other out. This can happen only if you, as the leader, empower and excite people for speaking their mind. Once they have that feeling of freedom, they also need to listen to each other. Not everyone is going to arrive at the same conclusion, but welcoming—and expecting—inquiry is part of supporting the critical thinking process. Here are some basic steps to support that. We'll go into these in more detail in chapter 9.

- Listen. When someone comes to you with an idea, take the time to really pay attention to what that person is saying without moving in to steer the conversation in the direction you want to go.

- Rephrase. Once a pitch has been made, rephrase it to make sure you understand it.

- Ask for confirmation or correction to make sure you've got the idea right.

- Ask for help in uncovering unstated assumptions. Examine how thoroughly the idea has been presented and ask, for example, where the idea was generated or what got the person thinking about the idea in the first place.

- Solicit counter-examples to see what reasoning works and, arguably more importantly, what doesn't.

DEVELOP

You and your team are experts at what you do. It took time to develop that expertise! There was not only the time on the job but also the years of education that provided you with some of the basic skills required to navigate through your daily life. No matter how talented you are, you can't become excellent at anything without training. Consider how long it takes someone to develop a musical or sports skill. A ballet dancer doesn't enter the world with strong muscles or practiced technique any more than a talented mathematician starts out knowing how to solve esoteric formulas. Developing critical thinking skills also takes time, despite the fact that each one of us is a thinker already. But just as an athlete must work hard to develop raw talent into skilled artistry, so, too, the thinker must develop rational processes. One of the best ways to do that efficiently is to focus on what you do best and to apply critical thinking concepts to those areas.

Let's suppose, as the owner of Flower Power—the fictional business we introduced in chapter 1—that you are an excellent floral arranger. Whether you're creating a wedding bouquet or a funeral wreath, you know what works for the occasion, season, client, and so forth. Unfortunately, you have trouble saying no to potential customers, and not because you want the work. In fact, you have too much work already, and you're worried that quality is going to suffer if you don't cut back or bring on additional help. Cutting back is difficult, because you can't bring yourself to say no. As for bringing on additional help, you don't have time to go through the rigorous process of advertising, hiring, and training someone to match your arranging style. It seems like you're stuck!

As Flower Power's proprietor, you have to determine what is and is not a good reason for taking on more work than you can successfully handle by yourself. If quality work is a value and part of your purpose, you need to find a way to preserve it. But with a bit more critical thinking, you may realize that there's another option, one that doesn't force you to dilute quality or spend valuable hours looking for additional help. For example, you could call around to a vocational college or similar institution that offers horticultural training to see if you can hire an assistant to help with prep work, such as cutting the flowers or preparing items needed for a certain design. This doesn't take long, and it doesn't require that you sidestep your purpose of providing quality arrangements.

Finding a way through the dilemma does not, however, solve your main problem. At some point you need to figure out why you have trouble saying no. It may be that you succumb to potential customers' emotional pleas—for example, arguments that use pity, fear, the desire to belong, and so forth. You need to be able to critically think through what someone is telling you and what you're basing your response on. Here are some examples:

Suppose you get pulled over for speeding. When the officer walks up to your window, you say, "Please officer, you can't give me a ticket. If you do, my insurance will go up, and I won't be able to afford my car anymore. Then I won't be able to get to work and I'll lose my job! I could get kicked out of my house if I can't pay my mortgage!"

Extreme? Yes, but it gives you an idea of what I'm talking about. If the officer gives in to your emotional plea, it's because he reasoned something like this:

This driver's life will be made miserable if I give her a ticket. I feel sorry for her. Therefore, I shouldn't give her a ticket.

But is feeling sorry for someone a good reason not to give that person a ticket when the individual has clearly broken the law? I doubt it.

Here's a slightly different version of the scenario:

"Listen, officer. You'd better not give me a ticket. I know the Chief. I'll get him to fire you!"

This time the extreme example reflects an attempt to coerce the officer, who reasons that this driver knows powerful people and will get him fired if he gives her a ticket. Therefore, he shouldn't give her a ticket.

An appeal to fear, like an appeal to pity, is not relevant to whether or not one should get a ticket for breaking the law. Let's look at one more version of the scenario:

"Come on, officer! I can't believe you stopped me. Look around. Everyone else is speeding, too. Why are you singling me out for punishment?"

If the officer concludes that he shouldn't give the driver a ticket because everyone else is speeding, there's faulty reasoning involved on both sides. After all, just because everyone else is doing (or not doing) something doesn't mean one should (or shouldn't) do it, too!

The point of all these stories is that you've got to develop serious critical thinking skills to focus in on your purpose, to communicate it to others, and to chart what you need to do to achieve it.

HONE

Once you have a sense of essential critical thinking skills, you need to refine them, beginning with consciously applying them to your daily interactions with others. Seeking out texts—including this book—that speak directly to questions you have and explore answers to those questions will also help lead you to new insights.

So, now that I've helped you begin to surface your critical thinking skills, turn to the next chapter where you'll learn to hone them.

CHAPTER 6

ACHIEVING YOUR PURPOSE THROUGH REFINED CRITICAL THINKING

I TRY TO ENCOURAGE PEOPLE TO THINK FOR THEMSELVES, TO QUESTION STANDARD ASSUMPTIONS . . . BE WILLING TO ASK QUESTIONS ABOUT WHAT IS TAKEN FOR GRANTED.
—*NOAM CHOMSKY*

Every day, each one of us makes decisions that impact our businesses at every level. Whether or not these decisions are any good, let alone support our values and our purpose, depends on how successful we are as critical thinkers. If we're good at it, we inspire confidence, encourage creativity, and understand the difference between risk and opportunity—and we can calculate how much of each of those it is reasonable to take.

Case Study: Critical Thinking During a Crisis—a Real-Life Example

Iron Mountain, Inc., a multinational, publicly traded company for whom I have worked, is a storage and information management organization that was established in 1951 by entrepreneur Herman Knaust. The company had a novel background: Knaust owned a depleted iron ore mine in New York that he originally used as part of a mushroom-growing business. After World War II, Knaust sponsored Jewish immigrants who had lost their papers during the war, which left them without proof of their identities. That got him thinking. He was also keenly aware of the public's growing anxiety over atomic safety. Acting on the idea of securing information, he created Iron Mountain Atomic Storage, Inc., and his mine became a facility for keeping sensitive documents of all kinds.

Fast-forward sixty years. In 2011, a tornado practically obliterated Joplin, Missouri. The "multiple vortex" tornado, which registered an astonishing 5 on the Enhanced Fujita Scale,[1] killed more than 150 people and caused almost three billion dollars in damages. Among the buildings affected was a hospital—an Iron Mountain customer— whose medical records were strewn around for miles, literally scattering private information everywhere. Sure, most of the city was initially concerned with rescue operations, but, as we all know, whenever there's a disaster, there are people waiting to swoop in and take advantage of it in any way they can.

When the Joplin tornado struck, the senior management at Iron Mountain pulled all their people together and sent them to Missouri. CEO William Meaney explained to me (and I later verified) the situation they faced and what they accomplished:

The task—collect every relevant piece of paper, no matter how damaged.

The challenge—overcome the environmental hazards in the aftermath of the tornado, such as chemicals and liquid fuels that had leaked from containers, fires that generated various toxins, and various waste materials and asbestos from damaged buildings.[2]

The solution—issue hazmat suits for all employees in the field.

The result—Iron Mountain's team recovered more than 90 percent of the hospital's records. Now that's information protection! There are many other Iron Mountain anecdotes like this one, all of which prove that their purpose of protecting their customers (and not just their information) dictates the company's actions.

The story reflects a business committed to living out its values. Iron Mountain is a publicly traded company, but that doesn't mean that investor profits trump those values. Instead, they are supported by those values, which the company refers to as "Taking CARE Pillars": Community engagement, employee Advocacy, information Responsibility, and Environmental sustainability.[3] When the tornado hit Joplin, Iron Mountain understood its purpose: to get to Joplin as fast as possible and recoup sensitive documents.

When Is a Promise a Promise?

Anyone who runs a business makes commitments—to employees, to customers, to clients. But even those companies with a clear purpose supported by solid values sometimes face a choice. Perhaps you broke your promise to complete a project for a client because a lucrative opportunity opened up and you couldn't do both. Or perhaps you could have completed a showcase assignment if only you had promised to take it on. How do you know exactly when you should make a promise and when you shouldn't?

It's not that easy. For one thing, none of us can predict the future. You can't know in advance what is going to happen. What makes promise-making and promise-keeping so tricky is that a promise is absolutely binding, but the world we live in is complicated. Imagine that you've promised to meet a friend for lunch. Lunch is no big deal, right? But you promised.

As you drive to the lunch meeting, however, someone hits your car. It's not your fault, but you won't make the lunch. Did you break your promise? What if you got a call from a prospective client shortly before noon, so you ditched your lunch plans with the friend, who also happens to be a client? Is breaking your promise because of a potential benefit a good justification?

As you can see, another aspect of the problem is determining whether or not the reason or justification you give for breaking a promise is a good one.

The critical thinker understands the difference between what is within our control and what's not. In addition, the critical thinker seriously contemplates the nature of a promise before it's made, so that she never makes a promise she is not confident she can live up to.

What about the promise broken because another opportunity comes along? The critical thinker recognizes that in that case you're going to lose your reputation, lose the trust customers have placed in you, and lose out on future opportunities. Whatever your purpose, people want to count on your word being as good as your actions. Critical thinking about the promises you can reasonably make—given the nature, size, and health of your organization—will clarify the difference between making a promise and saying you'll do the best you can.

So we see that critical thinking tied to our purpose involves not only carefully working through what to do and our reasons or justifications for doing so, but also how to do it. We can summarize it this way:

- Critical thinking is concerned with the types of decisions we make.

- Critical thinking is concerned with the reasons or justifications we provide for the decisions we make.

- Critical thinking is concerned with how we organize our reasoning.

Decisions and Justifications

Knowledge is crucial to making good decisions. I've spent these first six chapters talking about the importance of identifying and clearly articulating your values and your purpose. When you know what your values are and what your purpose is, you are in a much better position to make good decisions.

However, we often make decisions in the absence of complete information, and we often justify them by saying we want to avoid harming others. This seems like a good justification, especially for someone who evaluates the rightness or wrongness of an action based on the amount of good it produces and the harm prevented. But in this context, we have to distinguish between what we knew and what we could have or should have known. It's not reasonable to say that a decision is good only if it's based on complete information; that's rarely possible. Instead, we have concepts like due diligence and caveat emptor that provide those of us in business with formal frameworks for thinking about what would be sufficient information upon which to base a decision.

Duty, whatever the cost, is another way to justify one's decision to do or not do something. In this case, one's obligation is fulfilled when one acts from duty, so bad outcomes are lamentable but not things for which one is responsible. Suppose, for example, you jump into a pool to save a drowning child, but in the process of saving the child you break his arm. This is truly unfortunate but not something you intended to do; you acted from your belief that you must try to save the child, whatever the cost, and so the resulting broken arm is simply a sad result—collateral damage.

When we have a clear idea of what our organization's purpose is, we'll be less likely to enlist flawed justifications for our decisions. On the other hand, when we place our own needs before the purpose of the organization, we are more likely to make poor decisions. Making the right decision in those circumstances is probably accidental, since our justification simply fuels our own ego. The leader who takes credit for team members' work is obviously egotistical. A more subtle case is the leader who, wanting to be loved and appreciated, puts consensus ahead of tough decisions, often creating more strife and work than if the tough decision had been taken at the outset. In each case, a myopic focus is responsible for justifications that fail to support the organization's values.[4]

Howard Schmidt, vice president and general manager of Advanced Distributor Products, a division of Lennox International, clarifies the line a leader has to walk: "Asking for input is not the same as implementing it," he says. "At some point, the leader has to decide what to do." The leader is the one paid to make the tough decisions, not foist them off onto someone else or blame others for bad choices.

The crucial alternative to an ego-driven decision-making process is the critical thinker's detachment from his own emotions and from the self-interest that puts careful deliberation and quality decision-making at risk.[5] I'm not saying that the critical thinker is not entirely invested in the values and purpose on which he has carefully built his organization. Nor am I suggesting that the critical thinker doesn't care deeply about those values and purposes. But the critical thinker understands that he not only needs to look at problems and opportunities objectively and rationally to make good decisions but also to consider whether or not the justifications offered for those decisions are good.

Part of what makes a justification good is that it reflects what is actually the case. Of course, what's true—from events on the world stage to personal opinions—may shift from time to time. A lot of organizations make decisions based on focus group results. Sometimes a focus group can work, but when it doesn't, it's generally a major flop. Consider the rollout of New Coke in 1985—and how quickly it disappeared. That's because focus groups occur at a particular point in time. Suppose I'm a participant giving my opinion on some new product. I could have had a fight with my spouse and I would respond accordingly. Yet my opinion could color a company's long-term plans. All the more reason to have a firm grip on one's values and purpose.

We spend a lot of time justifying our decisions, especially those that may be controversial or not entirely accepted by others. This is exactly where critical thinking skills are most needed, and where the critical thinker can arrive at the best decisions after careful consideration of all the relevant evidence.

Organized Reasoning

Why is organized reasoning important? So you can clearly see how you arrived at your conclusion and whether it's good enough to support your purpose. In addition, systematically organizing your reasoning involves the careful consideration of all relevant evidence.

For example, you probably don't think much about how your car works until it stops working! The moment that happens, though, you engage in critical thinking. Let's suppose you get into your car, put the key into the ignition, turn the ignition, but nothing happens. All you get is silence. You try once or twice more, and then say in exasperation, "Great! Now I'm going to have to get a jump." Believe it or not, this statement is the result of a pretty complex reasoning process:

1. When nothing happens upon turning the ignition, either the alternator or the battery is "dead."

2. The interior lights don't work either.

3. Typically, when a car won't "turn over," the battery is dead.

4. Therefore, the battery is dead.

5. Therefore, I'm going to have to get a jump.

This is pretty standard stuff. The reasoning matches experience; it's not like I've suggested that elves have absconded with the battery. So far as I know, there's no experience that supports that conclusion!

We make all sorts of reasonable inferential leaps. Here's an example from watching a movie: In the film, a character walks toward a door to a building. He reaches out his hand. The scene then cuts to the character inside the building, closing the door behind him. We don't need to see the missing steps of walking inside and closing the door because, based on experience, we can mentally transition from one scene to the next.

So one approach to reasoning our way to a decision or conclusion is by way of experience. That may mean lived experience—what has happened in your life up to now. It can also mean a present sensory experience, like hearing the ticking sound of an engine failing to turn over. It can also mean tradition or inherited experience. Even if you've never had a dead battery yourself, undoubtedly you've heard about one. Similarly, it is unlikely that you've viewed earth from outer space, but you've certainly seen photographs taken by those who have.

Another approach to reasoning our way to a decision does not involve experience at all. Instead, it involves our intellectual ability to identify logical relations and come to a conclusion. Here's an example: There's an adorable series of commercials about California cheese involving talking cows.[6] At the end of each commercial there are two tag lines in cheddar-cheese-colored orange text: "Great cheese comes from happy cows. Happy cows come from California." Then the commercial ends. Your brain supplies the missing conclusion, which is that great cheese comes from California.

My point about reasoning independently of experience is important for a couple of different reasons. And, no, the example is not really about cows; it's about hundreds of little decisions you make every day. When you calculate—even something as small as determining the tip amount to leave your restaurant server—you're engaged in reasoning independently of experience. That's because numbers are not physical things you touch, taste, hear, see, or smell. Yet there's no question that reasoning correctly about numbers is very important!

Okay, let's pull a few ideas together to see how everything fits. Underlying this entire chapter is the idea that by honing your critical thinking skills you can identify your purpose, communicate it, and chart what you need to do to achieve it. It's a good idea to bear in mind that the ways you reason (either experientially or non-experientially) are just as important as the content of your reasoning (the stuff that you reason about).

Ideally, our reasoning is not just logically correct, but the content—the justification—is also true. That's why it's important that we gather good data. Recall the focus group discussion from earlier in this chapter. If you want the best shot at a good marketing campaign, you need good data. If you're using a focus group to collect that data, you want to make sure what you're gathering is accurate, and then you want to make sure you make a carefully reasoned decision about how that marketing campaign is going to look.

My point is that the content and the way you reason your way to a good decision impacts your success! Here's another way to think about this. What if you hired someone solely because the person dressed nicely during the interview, was friendly and outgoing, had a wonderful resume, and came already knowing a lot about your company? All these things are fine, as far as they go, but they aren't sufficient evidence for you to make your decision. If you fail to do your due diligence, such as running a background check or making sure the individual's actual skills match his or her resume, your decision may be flawed.

Another reason to talk about your critical thinking skills is to make you aware of what goes into your decision-making. You may be great at it without knowing why, but I submit that it's always better to know everything you can about what you do and how you do it—including the reasoning process behind your decisions.

One of the most significant contributors to your decision-making process is what gets it going in the first place. Arguably the most important feature of this process is what motivates your reasoning. Suppose that you are an empathetic person. You happen to be driving to an important meeting with a potential client when you see an accident. You could drive on by, but you also know that someone could be hurt. (You may also have a strong sense of duty and believe it's wrong not to stay to help, but let's suppose that this is not what you act on in this case.) Your empathy for others' welfare influences the decision you make and motivates you to stop.

Critical Thinking vs. Emotionally Driven Decision-Making

The bulk of our decisions—90 percent and more—are driven by emotion. That seems to undermine the idea that critical thinking, a rational process, is crucial to quality decisions. So how can we reconcile the two?

Philosophers, scientists, and theologians have long been interested in what drives people to do what they do and think what they think. Historically, they've separated motivations into two basic categories: feeling and reason. Research has shown that the two don't always work the way we want them to.

For example, the sort of empathy shown by the person who steps in to help a total stranger may mislead that same person to misplace empathy and be unfairly biased in another context. The results of a study published in a 2002 issue of the Harvard Business Review showed that accountants who conducted audits on companies with whom they had even a hypothetical relationship were more likely to find the company's financials in order. "Psychological research shows that our desires powerfully influence the way we interpret information, even when we're trying to be objective and impartial. When we are motivated to reach a particular conclusion, we usually do."[7]

Yes, we may be emotionally committed to our values, which may be born out of emotional states like empathy. However, this does not preclude us from using critical thinking to identify our values, discover our purpose, and become aware of instances in which our feelings are erroneously driving our decisions. I'm not saying you should become a Spock-like reasoning machine. After all, you are a human being with complex emotions. What I am saying is that you have to develop the skills that will help you reason your way to good decisions and avoid the pitfalls that generate bad ones.

Those skills will also help you build a culture as you surround yourself with people who share your values, as we'll see in the following chapters.

CHAPTER 7

SURROUND YOURSELF WITH PEOPLE WHO SHARE YOUR VALUES, BELIEVE IN YOUR PURPOSE, AND AREN'T AFRAID TO SPEAK THEIR MINDS!

DARE TO THINK FOR YOURSELF.

—VOLTAIRE

A 2012 *Forbes* magazine column entitled, "10 Reasons Your Top Talent Will Leave You," found the following:

- More than 30 percent believe they'll be working someplace else inside of twelve months.

- More than 40 percent don't respect the person they report to.

- **More than 50 percent say they have different values than their employer.**

- More than 60 percent don't feel their career goals are aligned with the plans their employers have for them.

- **More than 70 percent don't feel appreciated or valued by their employer.**[1]

These figures are significant and relevant to what I'm writing about in this book: People in the same organization have to share relevant values, and meaningful values are those that are integrated into all parts of your life. Let me tell you a story that explains what I mean.

Everyone Has Values; Who Shares Yours?

The CEO of a global company was attending its North American sales conference, at which I was the keynote speaker. After my presentation, he approached me and asked if we could have a cup of coffee. We sat down, and he proceeded to tell me his thoughts on my presentation.

"Scott, I believe in and agree with everything you said today regarding customer experience and emotional branding," he told me. "However, we are a manufacturing company and we are very process driven. It's difficult to get an entire organization to buy into a complete culture change."

I nodded, and he continued, "I have been the CEO for five years now, and my board members respect and like me. But as you know, a publicly traded company is very driven by earnings and shareholder happiness. I just don't know if I can convince them that the future of the company is to become customer-centric and shift from instant results to sustained results."

I smiled and said, "Didn't you just say that your board respects and likes you?"

"Yes," he answered decisively. "They do."

"Well," I went on, "if you believe in this, then tell them they need to believe in you."

He smiled, sipped his coffee, and said, "We'll talk."

Less than a year later, I was making a presentation at his company's global leadership conference in Europe, helping them to launch their new customer-centric culture! The CEO believed that the fundamental value that should direct the company toward achieving its purpose was the customer experience. Turning that into reality involved working with a board that shared his values.

A Shared-Values Case Study: My Ad Agency

Back when I ran my own ad agency, I had a major client who had a host of distributors for its product. At one point, we decided to run a promotion. Whoever bought a specific product from the company would receive an Exxon gas card as a perk. The client kept thousands of gas cards in a safe at my office, and each card was documented and accounted for. One of the distributors had a marketing director, a guy named Tommy, and he called one of my people, Dennis, who happened to be the director of this account as well as a number of others. Tommy asked Dennis to send over a slew of gas cards, but he wasn't real specific on what he planned to do with them. Dennis was stuck. He liked the guy, and he was responsible for keeping the client happy. At the same time, Dennis didn't want to disregard the process for dispensing the cards, let alone do anything unethical.

After deliberating about what to do, Dennis finally came to me and told me what Tommy had requested: "He said he'd take care of documentation, Scott, but I'm not sure if he's really going to give out the cards in the way we have things set up." Dennis was concerned that Tommy would give away the cards or somehow use them for his own purposes. I told Dennis not to send the cards to Tommy and to say he was not in a position to do so, knowing full well that this would put Dennis in a tight spot. Shortly thereafter, Tommy called the manufacturer and accused us of trying to rip them off. That didn't last long, however. Tommy's request was uncovered and he was fired, while we kept our account. Although I was intimately involved in my company, it was Dennis who had to go head-to-head with the marketing director. I knew when I hired Dennis that I had brought on board a man with integrity. And it was because Dennis shared my values that he made the decision he made.

That doesn't mean, though, that I automatically wanted everyone to see things exactly my way. That doesn't lead to a healthy company, either.

No "Yes Men" in Lincoln's Cabinet

It is a major understatement to say that Abraham Lincoln had a tough time during his presidency. Given that the country was on the brink of collapse and mired in the morally indefensible but still real fact of slavery, you'd think Lincoln would have sought shelter in a cabinet that would unconditionally support his plans and methods. Instead, as historian Doris Kearns Goodwin points out in *A Team of Rivals: The Political Genius of Abraham Lincoln*, the new president "made the unprecedented decision to incorporate his eminent rivals into his political family, the cabinet."[2] These men included his three rivals for the presidency: William H. Seward, who was appointed secretary of state; Salmon P. Chase, who became secretary of the treasury; and Edward

Bates, who was appointed attorney general. These men did not think Lincoln had the chops to be President of the United States, and they had tremendous political support of their own. Wouldn't they work to undermine his presidency, rather than support it? Why in the world would the president appoint them to his cabinet?

According to Lincoln, "We needed the strongest men of the party in the cabinet. These were the very strongest men. Then I had no right to deprive the country of their services."[3] These men were so strong, in fact, that eventually one of them—Seward—recognized Lincoln's greatness. "The president," he wrote, "is the best of us."[4] Bates, in contrast, never grew into the belief that the right man became president. Nevertheless, his animosity toward Lincoln paled in comparison to his belief that the United States should not be a nation of slave owners. And when Lincoln finally accepted Bates's resignation—something Bates had attempted several times before—he named Bates to the Supreme Court as its Chief Justice.

Lincoln maintained a balance among radical, moderate, and conservative viewpoints in the most important political positions he could appoint. There is no question that some of the core values of these men were different from their president's. But where it mattered most, there was sufficient consensus on fundamental values to move toward a common goal. And where there was insufficient consensus, the cabinet valued their president's utter steadfastness in pursuing his goals. Lincoln was a man of purpose. That purpose was clearly articulated; he did not waver from it, and his values clearly directed him toward achieving it. If nothing else, the President of the United States pulled together a cabinet that understood and shared this purpose as a value in itself.

Lincoln did not surround himself with yes men, and you shouldn't, either. That does not mean you should turn to contrarians or people whose core values are radically different from yours. Someone who disagrees just to be disagreeable—who says "no" to your "yes," but offers no argument in support of why "no" is the right answer—is not going to offer you robust discussion on how to move your business forward. And someone whose core values are radically different from yours is unlikely to find sufficient common ground to hash out ways to achieve your goals.

Suppose you do not believe that it is acceptable to cheat or steal under certain circumstances, but a potential employee does. How will you achieve your purpose together if you are wondering whether or not that individual will cheat or steal while in your employ or will promote those values in colleagues?

Of course, you shouldn't surround yourself with people who never question your plans or methods, who never critique an idea, or who never counsel you against taking a certain action; only a foolish person does that. Nor am I suggesting that you surround yourself with people who cannot provide you with quality support, either because they don't have the qualities required or because their values are opposed to yours. Part of great leadership includes creating a culture in your organization in which vigorous debate is welcomed, people's ideas are valued and genuinely considered, and no one feels insecure about speaking his or her mind, something we'll discuss at length in the next two chapters.

Who's Afraid of People Speaking Their Minds?

It takes a pretty confident person to create this sort of organization. The more confident you are about what you believe—and this is not the same as having an enormous ego—the easier it is to surround yourself with people who will challenge you to do your best work and share your purpose. You, in turn, will do the same for them. Confidence is also the result of careful critical thinking about what you believe is important and how to live in accordance with your values. This is arguably the heart of what makes a great and true leader.

That said, you've got to be comfortable with the fact that you don't always have to be the smartest person in the room. In fact, it's better if you surround yourself with people who are better than you are in significant ways. Success is not about your ego and making your employees suppress their own ideas so that you can look good! You don't want employees who are going to work harder at making an idea seem like it comes from you than at coming up with a stellar thought that benefits the entire organization.

People who are comfortable in their own skin are going to be comfortable around people who outshine them in various ways. And a good boss—a good leader, regardless of whether or not that person is in a supervisory position—is one who surrounds herself with the smartest, most capable people whose values align with hers. A good boss is going to be equally comfortable with having those values and the reasoning behind them challenged. That process only makes those values, and the results of realizing them in practice, better.

What happens if you are the sort of leader whose ego gets in the way? First, it's likely you won't hire people who challenge that ego, because you won't want the competition. And you won't surround yourself with people who are smart and sophisticated enough to see the gaps in your thinking, or they'll be too cowed to say anything. The end result is that your company will suffer. Moreover, you'll probably create a sort of shark-tank atmosphere where everyone is circling, waiting to make their move to get ahead. With their eyes on their prey and not the prize—achieving your purpose—the organization cannot survive.

A still-relevant 2002 *Fortune* magazine cover story, "Why Companies Fail," focused on the top ten reasons why businesses go under.[5] These included prolonged periods of success that led to complacency and a "fearing the boss more than the competition" attitude among employees. Supporting that conclusion, Daniel Goleman's *Primal Leadership* contains the results of studies that show how a subordinate's fear of a boss can stifle the sorts of interactions that are essential for good decision-making.[6]

The *Fortune* article also found fault with "listening to Wall Street more than to employees." (And, I'd add, listening to Wall Street more than customers!) No one knows a business like its employees. Ignoring them, as Lucent CEO Rich McGinn did in the late 1990s, had dire consequences: Lucent's scientists were interested in pursuing new optical technologies and its salespeople were concerned about the unrealistic growth targets McGinn had set. But the CEO's attention was on Wall Street and its love of his growth goals. After a short-term spike, the long-term result was an 80 percent stock plummet, and McGinn was out of a job.

Perhaps the two most profound observations in that *Fortune* article are that companies fail because their leaders are not self-reflective enough, and that failure itself is not merely a matter of going belly-up. The story's subtitle spells it out: "CEOs Offer Every Excuse but the Right One: Their Own Errors."

A Yes Men Case Study: The AIG Meltdown and a Turnaround

During the economic catastrophe of 2008, AIG, which insured against bad loans in the housing industry, and which had assets of over $1 trillion, was considered "too big to fail."[7] The US government ended up bailing out the company to the tune of $180 billion. But in more than one way, the company did fail. First, there was a failure of institutional coherence; the company's problems were so spread out it was hard to see that they were leading to disaster. Even worse, AIG's trading subsidiary, AIG Financial Products, engaged in unethical practices that included predatory lending practices, packaging substandard mortgages as investment opportunities, credit-default swap programs, and massive foreclosure rates. Apparently AIG's core value was making money, at all costs. As it turned out, the cost was somewhere around $180 billion.

Like pretty much everyone else, I was not only disappointed but also disgusted by the AIG meltdown. And while I understood the taxpayer bailout, I wasn't sure I agreed with it. I certainly didn't trust in the company to do the right thing.

It's easy to "see" values—good and bad—in others, especially in hindsight. It's much tougher, however—sometimes even arduous work—to identify our own core values in order to make connections between what we do on a daily basis at home, at work, with friends, and within our communities. When we do take that difficult step, however, lives are transformed. That is what happened at AIG under new leadership.

In early 2014, I was on a flight from New Orleans to Atlanta, and my seatmate and I got to talking, as strangers stuck on a flight often do. After exchanging pleasantries, I asked about work. She said, "I work for . . . " Then my seatmate, whom I'll call Pat, uttered something inaudible.

"Sorry, I missed that," I said.

"AIG. I work for AIG."

"Oh," I said. "Your voice kinda dropped off."

Pat laughed a bit and said, "I know. You never know how people are going to react when you tell them you work for AIG."

"I can understand that," I said. "A lot of people are still pretty gun-shy." After the bailout, the company had used some of the taxpayers' money to give outstanding bonuses to its management. The argument was that these were legally binding bonuses, but the fact that the very people who were allegedly responsible for the company's spectacular failures—financial and ethical—were not only offered, but also took, the money left a lot of folks angry.

"I know. I get it," Pat said. "But let me tell you about what's happening now. Things have really changed."

With the passion of someone who really believes in a leader and that leader's vision, Pat sat up tall, beamed with pride, and proceeded to tell me about Robert Benmosche, the CEO who took over in late 2009, after the company had gone through five chief executives in five years.

Pat confirmed news accounts that reported how Benmosche elevated morale at the company to the point where people could start to feel proud, not embarrassed, to work at AIG.[8] Of course, expression of such pride has been low key. The public doesn't forget so easily, and despite Pat's enthusiasm for her new CEO and the work he's done, it's understandable that people who don't know about these changes may be skeptical. I know I was. But after meeting Pat, my point of view has changed. The fact is, if you can take a reviled company like AIG and turn it around as Benmosche has done, you've got to be doing something right in the leadership department!

Under his guidance, AIG's stock not only doubled in value in two years, but the insurance giant has paid back every penny the US taxpayers loaned it, with interest—a lot of interest! Repaying what you owe reflects character in leadership. Staying on the job, despite enduring cancer treatments (as Benmosche has also done), reflects a commitment to something larger than himself. The government bailout saved a lot of jobs, but the values and purpose of this one man helped turn around a global company and made people feel good about working there again.

Your Values Are Your Business

Whether you're operating on the national political stage like Lincoln or the world financial stage like AIG, trust and reputation are created through words and actions. Say or do the wrong thing, and if it's serious enough, you can easily affect your business. I know this from personal experience.

I once sent the director and executive vice president of my ad agency to a meeting with one of our accounts. After just a few minutes, they were sent away. Shortly thereafter, I received a call from the client. I asked her how the meeting went, wondering why it ended so quickly.

She responded brusquely, "There was no meeting, Scott. I'm not interested in brainstorming with your employees; I want to brainstorm with you. In the future, if Scott Deming doesn't show up, I'm going to fire your agency."

I took a moment to gather myself, trying to figure out the best way to respond. I didn't want to be rude, but it seemed obvious that what she was asking for was impossible. "I'm so sorry to hear this, but please understand, this is a big company," I explained. "We've got lots of clients. I'm sure you understand that I can't be at every meeting."

"I'm not asking you to be at every meeting. I'm telling you I want you at every one of my meetings," she insisted. "I hired you."

You know what? For the most part, she was right. She knew that I knew my business and my company inside and out; I'd built it from the ground up. She also knew that I knew her industry inside and out, having worked in it for years. And she knew that I could make critical decisions concerning her account without consulting my boss, since I was, after all, the boss. These decisions were based on what I believed to be good and right, and they would immediately and positively impact her company's campaign and results.

My two directors, although bright and talented, did not give my client the feeling that she was in good hands, and that lack of confidence in my people was ultimately my fault. As hard as I tried, in this particular case, these two gentlemen either did not share my vision and values, or if they did, they were unable to convey that to the client. Ultimately, that is what made her uneasy enough to demand that I be involved at a level of detail I would otherwise leave to others in my organization.

The fact is that a CEO who comes in to run a company or a director who is hired to manage an account won't have the lived experience of someone who has started the organization from the ground up. Yet this person is in a leadership role! It is imperative, then, that this same individual not only share fundamental values with whoever hired him or her—whether it's me or a board of directors—but also have a clear idea of what those values are and how they will guide the employees toward realizing the organization's purpose.

The way to do that is by creating a robust company culture.

CHAPTER 8

A CULTURE FLOURISHES AROUND SHARED VALUES

IT IS UNDENIABLE THAT THE EXERCISE OF A CREATIVE POWER,

THAT A FREE CREATIVE ACTIVITY, IS THE TRUE FUNCTION OF

MAN . . . IT IS UNDENIABLE, ALSO, THAT MEN MAY HAVE THE

SENSE OF EXERCISING THIS CREATIVE ACTIVITY IN OTHER

WAYS THAN IN PRODUCING GREAT WORKS FOR LITERATURE OR

ART; IF IT WERE NOT SO, ALL BUT A VERY FEW MEN WOULD BE

SHUT OUT FROM THE TRUE HAPPINESS OF ALL MEN.

—MATTHEW ARNOLD

Loosely defined as the set of customs that reflect how we live together, culture is the expression of our values. In fact, there can be no culture without a shared commitment to those values, and that's true of business, too. If you do not have a clearly articulated set of values that guide your behavior as well as that of your colleagues, employees, and customers, it is unlikely you will be able to present a coherent identity and a clear direction, not only within the organization but also externally. As we've noted, values guide our collective direction toward our purpose, but it's nevertheless good to have different viewpoints on a single value to promote the sort of dialogue and brainstorming that leads to the best problem solving and planning.

And even if you've articulated your values to the people working in your organization, it doesn't mean you have provided them with a step-by-step manual of how to achieve them. Unless a value is absolute—never or always do X—there will be room for some discussion about how to realize these values on a daily basis. Knowing your values and your purpose and freely and creatively discussing how to achieve them is the sign of a healthy business culture.

The Davey Tree Expert Company: A Case Study in Creating a Flourishing Culture

A terrific example of a flourishing business culture comes from the Davey Tree Expert Company, (for whom I've worked). John Davey, an Englishman who immigrated to the United States in the late 1800s, was a pioneer in the science of tree surgery. Before him, there was no systematic thinking about, let alone practice of, how to deal with sick trees. In fact, the very notion of a sick tree was uncommon. Davey's abiding value was that natural resources should be preserved—especially those that, like trees, took decades to replenish. In 1880 he founded the Davey Tree Expert Company, which continues to thrive today in the United States and Canada as one of the largest privately held tree care companies in North America.

As for the company culture, it had its roots in something Davey's father told him when he was just a small boy. "Do it right or not at all," he'd advised.[1] Whatever "it" is, there is a right way and there is a wrong way. Never, the father admonished, do it the wrong way. If there is one right way of doing things, all you have to do is figure out what it is—no easy task. (Another reason why it's helpful to have a number of voices at the table.)

John Davey took his father's words to heart, and he elaborated on that basic value years later in a letter to his own son, Martin. And though the company is no longer family owned—in 1979 employees were offered and took advantage of an employee stock ownership program (ESOP)—the values set forth long ago remain the basis of the company culture. Though they seem commonsensical, they nevertheless highlight ways of balancing a profitable business with one's values and purpose. Here they are, with some of Davey's caveats and explanations.

"ABOVE EVERYTHING, MAKE YOUR WORD GOOD."

You should be judicious about the sorts of commitments you make. Whenever keeping your word is out of your control, you must straightaway tell the person to whom the promise was made.

"THINK OF YOUR CLIENTS BEFORE EVERYTHING."

Without clients, you have no business. Clients who "get honest value, quality workmanship, and diligent, conscientious service" are willing to "pay a fair price" for it. That, in turn, through good management, allows you to make "a moderate profit."

"IF A CLIENT MAKES A COMPLAINT, SEE THAT IT IS PROMPTLY AND FAIRLY INVESTIGATED."

The assumption is that clients are "good people" who wouldn't make false complaints. Anyone who does should be dealt with swiftly and then never served again. Assuming that people who complain believe they are in the right, the company should conduct its business accordingly.

"YOU CAN'T MAKE GOOD MEN OUT OF POOR ONES."
A business is not a "reform school," so its employees should not be those in need of reform. The best men are "diligent, careful, interested, and honest."

"TREAT YOUR EMPLOYEES AS HUMAN BEINGS."
The best men tend to be modest and so unlikely to push themselves forward as meriting reward. It is up to the business owner or manager to take note of and reward good work "before the employee has to ask for it."

"GOOD SALES REPRESENTATIVES SHOULD MAKE GOOD MONEY."
The good sales representatives are those who truly represent the company's "standards, principles, and ethics."

"WATCH YOUR CREDIT WITH A JEALOUS EYE."
Paying your bills, protecting your credit, and having enough money to cover payroll and all business expenses are paramount to staying in business.

"WATCH EXPENSES LIKE A HAWK."
Any money that is wasted must come from the clients, the employees, or the stockholders. Since that is not a company value, it must be avoided.

"WHEN IN DOUBT, DO NOTHING."

Decisions need to be made on a daily basis, but a snap decision lacks the sort of time required for thoughtful deliberation.

"YOU MUST MAKE A REASONABLE PROFIT."

A reasonable profit means your business stays afloat. A lack of profit means the business won't stay around for long, and exorbitant profit is likely the violation of at least one of the other values in this list. Moreover, a reasonable profit can be shared with the employees who helped make it possible.

"STAY OUT OF THE BANKING BUSINESS."

Lending money to anyone creates more work for the company and time away from the proper business at hand.

"NEVER DO ANYTHING WHILE YOU ARE ANGRY."

A calm, deliberative approach to business reflects having spent the requisite time thinking about things.

"PAY A MAN EVERYTHING THAT IS COMING TO HIM."

Whether a client overpays a bill or an employee submits an incorrect expense figure, "duty" demands accuracy.

"DON'T DO SOMETHING MERELY BECAUSE A COMPETITOR DOES IT."

Calm, judicial deliberation should drive merit-based decision-making, not other motivators.

"DO NOT TRY TO BE POPULAR IN YOUR BUSINESS DEALINGS."

As a business owner or manager, your job is to serve articulated values, not win popularity contests.

"TRY TO DESERVE RESPECT."

Although you are not in business to win popularity contests, "the solid qualities of character and old-fashioned virtues are of far greater importance than brilliance or shrewdness." If people know you are "just and fair and reasonable," they will respect you.

"BEWARE OF FLATTERERS."

Your motivation for making good decisions has nothing to do with flattery. Not only that, but flattery wastes valuable time and casts the flatterer in a suspicious light.

"SAVE YOUR OWN TIME."

Time is crucial to good deliberation and is required for you to prioritize successfully.

"DO NOT BURDEN YOURSELF WITH DETAILS."

Once again, time is a crucial element of success. Although you should know your company inside out, you should employ people who are reliable enough to handle the details in order for you to spend your time on specific priorities.

"IF YOU EXPECT OTHERS TO BE DILIGENT WORKERS, YOU MUST BE ONE YOURSELF."

As the head of the company, your work ethic sets an example for everyone in the organization.

"YOU OUGHT TO BE FRIENDLY IN A MODERATE AND RESERVED SORT OF WAY."

Genuine politeness "costs nothing" and displays respect for the person you address.

"YOU CAN NEVER COAST DOWN HILL."

Being "diligent, watchful, and active every day" will likely yield fewer problems than would arise if you simply sat back and enjoyed a successful period.

"INTELLIGENT AND PROPERLY HARNESSED, SELFISHNESS IS GOOD FOR MANKIND."

"Self-interest" and "selfishness" are used interchangeably here, and mean something like natural self-preservation. "All good business is founded on intelligent self-interest: that of the customer and the employee and the company." If a company is going to last, each interest should be reasonably served.

"IT IS WELL TO WORK EARNESTLY TOWARD PERFECTION."

Although impossible to achieve, perfection must be our goal. In "working earnestly" to achieve it, your business will be better off than if you did not, for "[t]he natural pull of human inertia and indifference is downward." Pulling in the other direction requires a certain unspoiled moral courageousness.

John Davey's advice may not click with you, but whether or not your values align with his, you can see that he has given each concept thoughtful consideration. And that's exactly what I've been asking you to do, both explicitly and through discussions of how we make sense of our values theoretically.

Davey also was more specific than we typically are in articulating business values. It is remarkable, however, that his tenets gave rise to a viable and long-lasting company culture. Although over the years many different ideas, methods, and approaches were used to achieve the Davey mission and purpose, the core values never changed.

A Culture of Creativity Case Study: SAS's Jim Goodnight

If the company culture expressed by the Davey Tree Expert Company strikes you as a bit old-fashioned, it's useful to look at a very up-to-date example. Jim Goodnight established SAS, his software company, based on personal values and a clear purpose: to create topflight software and services that aid the management and analysis of increasingly large data sets.[2] The intellectual power and creativity required to accomplish these tasks is at the core of the company's purpose, which Goodnight, himself a former statistics professor at North Carolina State University, sets. A leader in every sense of the word since the company's founding in 1976, Goodnight and his enterprise have become models for others to emulate and study. SAS is considered to be the Harvard of corporate America. People want in; they apply in droves for few openings.

For Goodnight, valuing employees in tangible ways is one expression of working toward his purpose. For example, SAS offers in-house day care, original art hangs on the company walls, and people have the freedom to use their time as they see fit. All these gestures contribute to a culture that puts a premium on individual creativity, inspired by a belief in each employee's worth as a human being—that's the organization's primary value.

In a 1998 interview with Fast Company magazine, Goodnight said, "Creativity is especially important to SAS because software is a product of the mind. As such, 95 percent of my assets drive out the gate every evening. It's my job to maintain a work environment that keeps those people coming back every morning. The creativity they bring to SAS is a competitive advantage for us."[3]

For Goodnight, there is a symbiotic relationship between his commitment to see his business succeed and promoting intellectual creativity, and that has both contributed to the corporate culture and led to its success. Since its founding, SAS has grown into a multibillion-dollar company. The company grew from $138,000 in profits its first year to more than two billion dollars in 2010, and not once in its history has there been a layoff.

A Culture of Routine Excellence Case Study: US Display Group

I interviewed Dennis Mehiel, CEO of U.S. Display Group, on my inaugural podcast of SuccessCast.[4] Dennis has had a long and successful career in the packaging business, having worked his way up through the ranks since the age of fourteen, when he started cleaning offices, to become CEO of U.S. Corrugated. He still works in corrugated-box manufacturing.

From the beginning, Dennis's dad told him starting at the bottom would build character. At the time, Mehiel didn't believe him. Years later, he's changed his mind. He sees the value of learning the business inside and out. "Nobody that ever worked with me . . . at any level of the organization did not at some point know what my background was and know that I knew the business at that level and what that kind of work was like." For Mehiel, understanding the business from the ground up meant he was able to connect with employees at a level that those without his experience could not do.

The values Mehiel developed while working through the ranks informed the decisions he would later make as a corporate leader. Those decisions are guided largely by the fact that his company's relations with clients are ongoing; the company's mission is to serve clients continuously. Mehiel expects to develop relationships that last decades. This requires a more intensive commitment to one's values on the part of everyone in the organization than does a "one-off" approach that you might find at, say, an interstate truck stop where the vast majority of the business comes from single-visit customers.

So I asked him how he keeps morale up and keeps people coming back to work every day with the desire to make things happen for the company. "How do you talk to people to make them feel like they're a part of something special?" This is the foundation of a corporate culture, and it's an especially tricky question to put to someone who runs a company that makes boxes and point-of-purchase displays—cases for things like candy and potato chips. How do you get excited about making boxes?

But Mehiel not only takes the question in stride, he welcomes it, because it gives him a chance to articulate the values he believes permeates the entire company.

"That's really the essence of leadership," Mehiel responded enthusiastically. "The vast, vast majority of people that have worked in our company over the years, or in any company, are doing this to support their family. They're doing this because they need a paycheck. To create a culture and a workforce that really feels bought into something that feels important, that's really the essence of leadership. We're not curing cancer when we're making corrugated boxes, and that's not lost on anybody, right? But what we are doing is providing a place where people can safely earn a living, where people can support their families—and we are taking care of a very important need that a tremendous, uncountable number of companies have."

One of Mehiel's companies makes boxes for packaging or shipping. When you buy something—say, a blender at Target—or have something shipped to you—perhaps a clock from Amazon.com—it typically comes in a corrugated box. Manufacturing these boxes is what Mehiel's company does, and that's even less glamorous than making point-of-purchase displays! He understands that in some ways, what happens at his company feels unimportant, or at least disconnected from life-or-death work. Nevertheless, Mehiel's companies do have articulated values that are promoted throughout the organization every day.

It would be easy to say that a company that designs and manufactures point-of-purchase displays doesn't need to concern itself with identifying, living, and promoting values. Yet on the landing page of U.S. Display Group's Web site is this bold claim: "We are a dynamic, high-energy company that is built around people, values, and teamwork."

The company also has a financial goal, to be sure. Nobody starts a company hoping it won't make money! But a company whose values include employee safety, security, and responsibility is a company whose values drive it in ways a purely money-driven enterprise cannot and whose values help the corporate culture flourish.

Mehiel elaborated on the value of individual responsibility and the meaningfulness of individual contributions to making the business a success. "What I've experienced over the years in our business is that people like it when an order comes in on Tuesday afternoon, and it's impossible to deliver it by Wednesday afternoon, but the customer screwed up, and this is a desperate situation, and so you kinda move heaven and earth a little bit and bail the customer out. And maybe they write you a thank-you note, and maybe they don't, but either way, your people know what they did and are invested in what they're doing. Let's remember that most people's default setting is that they want to do a good job, they wanna work hard, they wanna be part of a winning team. That's one of the fundamental things for me: always helping people feel like they're playing for a winning team, because then people will stand up a bit taller and work a bit harder. The first thing people want to know is that you care about their physical health and well-being and that you value them as a person."

For Mehiel, safety was always ahead of profit, and he generated a culture that reflected that value. Mehiel is also convinced that this should be a core value for everyone.

He's not alone. As part of my research for a presentation I gave on how certain values shape businesses in positive ways, I came across a Gallup study in which the fifth-most important reason for someone to want to remain with or leave a company is whether or not that employee is valued as a person. That's what Mehiel does. That's what Jim Goodnight at SAS does. That's what any good leader does.

Changing the Culture

Howard Schmidt, the vice president and general manager of Advanced Distributor Products whom we met in an earlier chapter, believes that a company's culture flourishes when it taps into people's desire to be part of something that is working well and making a difference. But what happens when a change in culture is required? That's a difficult process, acknowledges Schmidt. It's hard enough for an individual to change, let alone an entire group.

Howard Schmidt recognized that ADP needed to move away from the typical manufacturer marketing and selling process if the company was going to be an industry leader. He knew they needed to be more about solutions and less about product. However, many people in the organization were already part of the "old" process, and changing their thinking and their approach would not be easy. How to go about it? The best way to understand a current company culture and to move employees to buy into changing values and circumstances is to spend time listening and talking to people in all areas of that organization. What do they love and not love about their company? What seems to be working and not working with the current process? Can they articulate the values and purpose that will guide the company in the future? How willing are they to accept change?

When Schmidt began the process of change at ADP, he initiated monthly formal and informal review meetings that included leaders from across the organization. Executives, managers, and non-senior employees who were well regarded all got to hear and contribute to the same story about change in the organization. Consequently, everyone knew what was happening, why it was happening, and how they would participate and be affected. "We don't change any significant projects unless everyone buys into it," management said. This approach extended to other environments in Schmidt's organization, from the sales force to customers to those on the factory line. Nevertheless, Schmidt was aware that as change began to occur, some people would find that the new culture did not reflect their values, and they would leave.

Throughout the process, four core values emerged to drive the organization: integrity, fulfilling commitments and promises, respect for others, and a devotion to excellence that makes innovation possible. Those who remained with the organization or who later came on board shared those values and the company culture.

Let's turn to your business. How can you incorporate what these leaders have done to create your own strong corporate culture? The next chapter addresses that question.

CHAPTER 9

HOW TO BUILD A FLOURISHING CULTURE AROUND YOUR VALUES

First they came for the Socialists, and I did not speak out—
Because I was not a Socialist.
Then they came for the Trade Unionists, and I did not speak out—
Because I was not a Trade Unionist.
Then they came for the Jews, and I did not speak out—
Because I was not a Jew.
Then they came for me—and there was no one left to speak for me.
—Martin Niemöller

Martin Niemöller was a German pastor and theologian in Nazi-era Germany. The poem that I cite in the epigraph is famous for its power to evoke a sense of moral outrage at what Hitler and his henchmen did to millions of people before and during the war. What most of us cannot understand is how any of it was able to happen. How did a culture of hate and violence become so entrenched and so public in such a short span of time?

I'm not a history scholar, and I do not pretend to have some grand theory about the aftermath of World War I or some psychosocial account of the German zeitgeist. What I do know is that a culture cannot flourish if individuals do not sustain it. Whether it's a beautiful or horrific culture, it does not exist without one individual after another choosing to support it. In other words, if one person after another shifts away from a set of practices and beliefs that are the core of any culture, that culture eventually ceases to exist. This doesn't mean there is no society or company, but that surely the culture has vanished.

It's All About You . . . and You, and You . . .

As we've seen, you are at the heart of your values. You are the core of your purpose. Why? Because you, and you alone, are the one who chooses for yourself. Not only that, but your purpose is the goal of your collective values, and you choose your values.

Sure, there are some things that influence what you do, and others that even dictate it. Systems, bureaucracies, policies, rules, regulations, laws, and other individuals impact your life. But whatever your situation and however you were raised, when it comes time to choose who you are and who you want to be, it all comes down to you. You are the one who envisions which way your organization is headed or how to change course, if necessary. You may be the one who can solve a problem that keeps a client from jumping ship. You may be the one with a great idea like Bill Gates, Steve Jobs, or someone who wins a Nobel Prize. You may be the one whose mentoring changes lives for the better.

You also know that although you are responsible for choosing your values, what you do next is going to involve more than just you. In other words, you and multiple other individuals will make the difference between a culture that lasts and one that does not.

Now, however, I want you to start thinking pragmatically about how to build the flourishing culture you want in your organization. Specifically, I want to focus on some essential concepts and a step-by-step process for creating and maintaining that culture.

For me, the culture that I want to live and work in is achieved through what I value most: values like honesty, fairness, and promoting success for everyone involved in and related to my organization. These are among the values that guide me to my purpose, which is helping people realize their best selves. What follows are ten steps you can use to create a similar culture for your organization:

Step 1. Create Stakeholders: It Begins and Ends with You

If you are recruiting people into an organization that reflects a carefully articulated purpose and set of values, you've got to begin and end your day thinking about and acting on those values. You are the one who sets the tone for the culture you're trying to create—and it's obvious by now that I don't mean by deciding whether to wear jeans and a t-shirt or a suit and tie to work every day! It starts with the way you interact with each person at every level within your organization and outside it. **Make sure your values and purpose are known to everyone and that they provide a core framework for daily operations.**

You can create, for example, a code of ethics to which you clearly adhere and expect everyone else to follow as well. Consider the 2013 brouhaha over the policy set by Yahoo's new CEO, Marissa Mayer, who proclaimed that employees had to work in the office as opposed to remotely. She was clearly taking a controversial tack toward changing both the culture and productivity levels at Yahoo, and she was both roundly criticized and highly praised for her efforts.[1] The people who stick with that plan over the long haul are those who share Mayer's vision for the company.

Step 2. Create Stakeholders: It's Not Enough to Bring People on Board

It's not enough for you to bring people on board who share your values and your purpose. You need to keep these people on board. In most cases, if you're charismatic, passionate, and compelling enough, you'll be able to sell something to someone, whether it's a product, service, or a position within your company. The real challenge, however, comes with holding on to the client or the talented employee. So what's the formula? Let me be clear that it does not involve a constant state of inspiration. Those big movie moments are really few and far between, and anyway, the sort of energy it would take to sustain them would run you down in short order.

The formula for sustaining long-term engagement does, however, involve a fair amount of work. That's because it requires being consistently genuine. Depending on the size of your organization, you should have regular, organization-wide meetings where people can share best practices, learn about what others' jobs are like, and discover how areas of the organization overlap. If you are part of a very large organization where company-wide meetings are not possible, then be sure to arrange for regular departmental meetings and some sort of annual organization-wide gathering. Remember that you want people who will actively engage with you and each other without fear of your ego getting in the way. But part of that active engagement requires that people have at least a basic understanding of how the different areas of the organization fit together.

One of the biggest challenges in running my advertising agency was getting people in different departments not only to understand what the other people in other areas did, but also to appreciate the work. For example, our account executives and account coordinators were solely responsible for keeping the client informed and happy. They were the face of the company. They were responsible for keeping their programs on schedule, which meant they had to provide pertinent information to the client for approval, such as creative samples, media proposals, and costs for production. If they promised a client they would have the media plan to them within a week, they did so, not knowing what it took for the media planners and buyers to get accurate and cost-effective information. If they promised the client a creative briefing within two weeks, they did so, not knowing what other jobs were already in the creative department's queue and how long it actually took to come up with great ideas. The creative and media folks, on the other hand, never really worked directly with clients; therefore they did not understand how demanding and inflexible some of them could be.

As you can imagine, there was a lot of stress and frustration on both sides. The solution? We created a cross-training or cross-pollination program, in which, periodically, everyone in the agency had to spend a week working next to someone from a completely different department. Account executives would sit in on creative meetings or listen in on the negotiation process the media buyers went through. Creative types would sit in on client meetings and calls to better understand what the account people had to deal with on a daily basis. This program helped to create a greater understanding within our company from department to department and from person to person. It also eliminated an awful lot of fighting and finger-pointing!

Just a few months ago I was the keynote speaker for a large, international bank. I also created and monitored a two-hour breakout session that was titled, "Perception is Reality." The exercise during the session was the same as the cross-pollination process I describe above, and it was created for many of the same reasons—to facilitate a better understanding of what others do and to eliminate fighting and finger-pointing within the organization, which was beginning to run rampant. At this bank, from department to department, there was the same lack of understanding of what others did and what reasonable expectations should be. During this breakout session, loan originators learned from loan processors, who learned from underwriters, who learned from the credit department, and so on.

My guess is that these issues occur within your organization as well. If so, do yourself and your company a big favor and start educating people on what others at the same company do every day. It will create realistic expectations, eliminate assumptions, and create a more harmonious, productive, and profitable environment.

Step 3. Promote Accountability: Freedom, Transparency, and Responsibility

Eleanor Roosevelt said, "With great freedom comes great responsibility." When you create the sort of culture that encourages people to share and challenge ideas, you create a culture in which people feel free to innovate and be creative. This also means that people are responsible for what they say and what they do. We all are agents of our actions.

On the positive side, being responsible means giving people credit for the work they do. On the negative side, being responsible means identifying the source of an error, being willing to own up to it, and, more importantly, taking the steps to fix it. If people aren't free to say what they think, they're also less inclined to take responsibility for things that go wrong and to be resentful of not getting praise for things that go right.

Now bear in mind that just because you work to create a culture of openness, you should not expect complete transparency. In an age of decreasing privacy but increasing accountability, you have to understand what is for public consumption and what is not. Technology writer Douglas Rushkoff, in a piece about technology and transparency, illuminates my idea in an interesting way that goes beyond an example to the heart of the contemporary tension between being open and having your privacy invaded.

Rushkoff points out some disturbing Facebook practices that made him question that organization's values.[2] Facebook, he contends, "actively misrepresents us to our friends, and worse, misrepresents those who have befriended us to still others." For those of us who use the app as a convenient way to reconnect and maintain contact with friends and acquaintances, what Rushkoff tells us should give us pause: "Facebook does not exist to help us make friends, but to turn our network of connections, brand preferences, and activities over time . . . into money for others." One of the questions we need to ask is whether or not we are being ill-used by the company. Let's examine this more closely in light of how technology factors into our interactions.

Advances in technology are such that huge—enormous—data sets are both available and interpretable as never before. As Rushkoff points out,

> We have been handing over to [Facebook] vast quantities of information about ourselves and our friends, loved ones and acquaintances. With this information, Facebook and the "big data" research firms purchasing their data predict still more things about us—from our future product purchases or sexual orientation to our likelihood for civil disobedience or even terrorism.

When you visit Amazon.com, you'll see that your history of searches has been preserved, and Amazon provides you with suggestions based on those searches. Most any commercial site will be able to track a user in such a way that previous searches yield specific advertisements on those sites. For example, if I search for a good deal on Crocs shoes at the Crocs site, I suddenly find Crocs advertisements practically everywhere I go! You know what it's like when you shop online and then start receiving massive quantities of advertisements from companies that have purchased your contact information and probably also your purchasing preferences. It's creepy! You probably feel like you're being followed—and you are. An entire industry has built up around data collection and mining for the express purpose of running algorithms that aim at predicting what you might do next, so that businesses can be there waiting for you.

I'm sure I'm not telling you anything you don't already know. And these types of activities are the reasons it's difficult to create an atmosphere of transparency in the workplace. People don't automatically trust others, and that's a direct result of companies big and small duping people into thinking they're doing one thing but in reality doing something completely different. If you are going to create an environment and a culture of trust, transparency, and honesty, you must live it every day and not just preach it. You must say the things you believe are true, and you must do the things you say you will do. Paying lip service to customer service, for example, without living up to the promises you make undermines trust. You can only "cry wolf" so many times before people stop believing in what you say.

Step 4. Create Dialogue: Listen

Related to the idea that a vibrant culture is one that encourages people to speak their mind and expects the experience to be beneficial for everyone involved is the idea that people should take dialogue seriously. Believe it or not, many people don't know how to have a conversation that actually produces good ideas. Lots of times, we don't listen to each other but rather simply wait for our chance to get our point across.

Listening may be hard to do, but it's especially important when you're the one who's setting the tone for the organization's culture. You may want to ask a question for clarification or if you've lost the thread of what someone's trying to say, but start by listening. In particular, concentrate on what the person's point seems to be and why he or she thinks that way. They'll almost always tell you.

It's often the case that what we hear is not what the person said or meant to say. Take time to reformulate someone's thoughts in your own words. You can say something like, "What I hear you saying is . . ."

The point of really listening is to understand and, more often than not, to take action on what you hear. You need to build a reputation for just this sort of behavior. If you don't, you'll cut yourself off from the very people whose experiences you need to know about—employees and customers!

There's a Wharton Business School article that tells a familiar story about unsatisfied customers complaining to others about their experiences, and how this sort of word-of-mouth can be devastating for any organization.[3] That's partly because when people talk to each other, stories are embellished with each retelling and also partly because people seem less inclined to complain to the organization directly. They don't believe the organization will listen to them, let alone do anything about it. But when you run a business, the last thing you want to do is create an experience that disappoints your customer. That person will tell everyone about it, even if they never say a word to you!

Step 5. Create Dialogue: Confirm or Correct

Ask the person you're speaking with to confirm that your recapitulation of their meaning is accurate, or to correct you. After all, the ideas you're trying to get right are theirs, not yours. Yes, the one communicating has the burden of making him- or herself clear, but you can help improve the person's articulation. In addition, since you want people to take responsibility for what they say and do, you need to know you've got it right, and you need them to know that you care about that.

Take some time to listen to a disagreement between two people. See if you can find out its source. People disagree over facts, but more often than not, their disagreements are just verbal. Here is an example:

Person 1: I believe that everyone is created equal.

Person 2: What are you talking about? People all have different DNA!

Person 1 has made a moral claim about people's equal value. Person 2 doesn't address the issue about people's equal value. Instead, Person 2 interprets "equal" in a biological sense. Instead of disagreeing with Person 1, Person 2 could restate Person 1's position to see whether or not Person 1 agrees. Alternatively, Person 1 could potentially avoid the dispute by more clearly articulating the type of equality intended.

Step 6. Create Dialogue: Situate the Conversation

See if you can situate what someone is saying within the organization's established framework of values, and try to find a connection or some alignment with the organization's purpose. Doing so will help keep the focus on why everyone showed up for work!

Noted management consultants Dr. George Labovitz and Victor Rosansky have written about what alignment means in an organization:

> Alignment is a condition in which the key elements of an organization—its people, strategy, customers, and processes—work in concert to serve its primary purpose . . . Whatever the enterprise or its goals, the degree to which those key elements are integrated and working in concert will determine how quickly and successfully it will fulfill it [sic] primary purpose.[4]

The authors don't focus specifically on values, but the model applies to these as well as to the strategic interests of the organization. The authors also point out that alignment—which I'm proposing occurs by way of dialogue at the level of the organization's framework of values—cannot be self-sustaining. Instead, people have to keep working at it. This is why quality, continuous dialogue is essential to creating a culture that reflects your values.

Step 7. Create Dialogue: Consider Assumptions

Every story has to begin somewhere; we have to assume something to get things going. Similarly, when we engage in dialogue, we make certain assumptions that are often not explicit. They're simply the givens we take to be true for the purpose of starting. Just as you do when you reformulate in your own words, check with the speaker to see if what you believe they have assumed is, in fact, what they assume!

As with verbal disputes, it's often the case that our disagreements occur because of what is not said. In other words, we don't state our assumptions, and we believe we know what others' assumptions are, but we're wrong!

Step 8. Disagreement Does Not Mean Stalemate: Give Others' Ideas a Try

One of the political tactics both Republicans and Democrats use is to actively undermine their opponent. Even if the other guy or gal has a good idea, the opposing side reflexively and staunchly opposes it. Why? Because they don't want to see the other side win. Ever. It's no wonder the state and federal governments are about as innovative and efficient as a slug. Sorry . . . slugs actually deserve a bit more credit than that!

If you and someone in your organization disagree over an idea or a process but a decision is made to implement it, make sure everyone gives it the same support they would show if they thought it was the best thing since sliced bread. It's your job to get people on board and excited about the direction of a program, process, or policy, whether it was your idea or not. It's easy to help things fail; it's a lot harder to see them succeed. Since everyone in your organization is after the same thing, it is in everyone's best interest to try to make implementing others' ideas work.

Step 9. Change: Manage It

People have been talking about change management for decades.[5] The fact is, like everything else in life, a company is fluid, and it changes daily. Companies implement new software, new policies, hire new people, bring on new vendors and clients, and so on. Companies change in response to both internal and external stimuli.

Change is a scary, scary thing for most people. They don't know where they fit in with this change, or if they'll be left out. It's important, therefore, that whenever change is on the horizon, those who are responsible for deciding to implement it communicate their reasons clearly and thoroughly. People need to understand the context for change as well as how change will impact their workload, workflow, planning, and so forth. Continuous dialogue sustains organizational values and in so doing facilitates positive change. It's important to work at maintaining the thread of those values throughout or across that change.

Here are some ways in which you can capitalize on that dialogue as you manage changes large and small:

- Remember that, in fact, it's not actually organizations but individuals who change. To the extent that, for example, an organization moves location or upgrades technology, it may be said to change. But none of this change occurs by itself. Individuals make these—and all things that go on in an organization—happen.

- Organizational leadership is that which both facilitates and inspires positive individual and sustainable change.

- Understand that effectively managing individual and organizational change will have a direct impact on organizational results.

- Do not be afraid of resistance to change! It is natural, and it is possible to both anticipate resistance and mitigate its negative effects by planning for it and making that plan a core element of the change itself.

- Even when individuals can align a change with their own self-interest and belief system, the uncertainty of success and fear of the unknown can block change and create resistance. The question, therefore, is not if we will encounter resistance to change, but rather how we support stakeholders through the change process and both fairly and equitably manage that resistance.

- People generally resist change when:

  - They were not part of designing it;

  - They don't know why it's happening;

  - They do not believe the reason for it is valid;

  - They do not trust the messenger;

  - They are uncertain about how the change will impact them, both personally and professionally.

- Be patient with individuals who are working their way through the change process, and enable your team to become effective change leaders.

- Offer training as needed or requested and attempt incremental changes, but make sure they don't seem arbitrary. For example, a software upgrade is an incremental change, but it's made within the context of existing software use; it doesn't appear out of nowhere.

- Make sure the steps in the change process, as well as the reason for the change, are understood by all, both in terms of the organization's current structure and work and in terms of individual classifications.

- Most important, make sure changes are in keeping with the organization's purpose and values, so that there is continuity on which everyone can rely.

Step 10. Values: You're in the Relationship Business

Never forget that human interactions are always meaningful at some level. You've probably had interactions that, for some reason, were really meaningful to others, though you thought them to be rather pedestrian. And the shoe has likely been on the other foot, too. You can never anticipate what is going to impact someone else's life in a really meaningful way, but be aware that it's always possible. If your interactions reflect your values, then you can always be confident that you have contributed to creating a meaningful culture wherever you go.

CHAPTER 10

DO ONLY WHAT SUPPORTS YOUR VALUES AND ACHIEVES YOUR PURPOSE

Your beliefs become your thoughts,

Your thoughts become your words,

Your words become your actions,

Your actions become your habits,

Your habits become your values,

Your values become your destiny.

—Mahatma Gandhi

So far we've discussed identifying our values and purpose and understanding how to create a robust culture based on those things. We live in the real world, however, and it's not always easy to maintain our focus in the face of the demands made upon businesses. Yet it is possible. Consider, for example, the story of Chipotle Mexican Grill, for whom I have worked in my capacity as a corporate speaker.

Chipotle Knows What Supports Its Values: A Case Study

As I do with all of my clients, I researched the company and found that Chipotle was founded on strong values and purpose, which are integrated at all levels of the organization. If I don't believe in a company, I don't do business with them.

Restaurant founder and co-CEO Steve Ells wanted to create a chain of restaurants "where you could eat delicious food made of the finest ingredients quickly and affordably."[1] He believed the key component of delicious food was that it be made from the finest ingredients. But where do you get those, and how in the world can you make affordable food from it? We all know why most fast food is so cheap: It's made using industrially produced materials, from the animal products to the tomatoes that go on the burgers. The problem with industrial farming, Ells found, however, is that it's not only ethically dubious but it's also not always particularly healthy or conducive to a sustainable environment.[2] As Ells tells it, there had to be "a better way." He wanted to find ranchers and farmers "dedicated to raising livestock and growing produce using responsible, respectful, and sustainable techniques."

Okay, so Ells had a multifaceted purpose: creating affordable, quickly prepared, delicious food made from the finest ingredients. He also had a set of values that included reliance on environmentally sustainable and ethical food production. He could have compromised. He could have made food that tastes great and is made quickly but isn't made entirely from the "finest ingredients." He chose not to do so. His decision has paid off. Today Chipotle is one of Fast Company's 50 most innovative businesses in the world.[3] In 2006 Chipotle went public, and the stock was up more than 400 percent in 2010—just four years after its initial IPO.[4] In 2012 co-CEOs Steve Ells and Monty Moran earned terrific compensation packages and stock gains.[5] Not bad for a company that refused to waver from its purpose and values!

Part of knowing what supports your values involves knowing your business; good choices are well informed. Ells already knew a lot about food production and preparation. When it came to aspects of the business world he didn't know, he brought in Monty Moran as co-CEO. Trained as a lawyer, Moran was initially Chipotle's general counsel; then he became president and COO. He'd been with the company from its earliest days, was clearly committed to the organization's values, and had worked closely with Ells to scale those values to fit its growth. In short, Moran knew the company well enough to make sound judgments on how to facilitate realizing its purpose.

Aligning Values and Purpose: A Case Study

As you can see, values can align with purpose, but figuring out how to do that may require critical thinking and difficult soul searching, especially in a global economy.

Consider the following hypothetical scenario.[6] A manager of a large US company has been assigned to open up a division in China. She has recently been promoted, and the new division and its success is her responsibility. A Chinese native who has spent her entire adulthood in the United States, she's an expert on both Chinese and US business practices. So, although she's excited to have the opportunity to return to China, she is also concerned about doing a good job, which is complicated.

Specifically, she is concerned about how to navigate the system in her native country. She knows that there are particular difficulties with doing business in China; as recently as 2013, the country was known for such things as corruption[7] and human rights violations.[8] From what she's heard, it seems like business doesn't get done there unless you pay bribes or mistreat workers. She wonders if she'll have to adjust her values, which align with those of her company, in order to be successful. What should she do?

Suppose you were in her position. Would you have a discussion with the company's executives? Would you compromise until you had established your firm's presence in China?

Now suppose you're her boss, the CEO of the company. What's your responsibility? Do you sit down with her before she leaves and review the reality of doing business in China and your expectations? Do you give her the authority to make decisions on behalf of the company? Are you willing to break off the project if it becomes clear you can't maintain your values while establishing a successful presence in China? These are among the questions you need to consider.

The fact is, doing what's right is almost always harder than not doing it, while doing something that isn't right can be pretty tempting. In business, this difficulty seems to be compounded by the ultimate temptation—money—and, in many cases, the ultimate responsibility, shareholder happiness. Boards and CEOs will often make the wrong decisions, such as eliminating a positive customer experience, to make quarterly profits. These sorts of behaviors reflect a focus on the next three months, not the long term, and ultimately harm the customer, the employee, and the company itself.

One Woman's Story: A Case Study About Derailed Purpose

Let's look at a couple of cases in which the purpose and values of a large organization got lost in the pursuit of shortsighted goals. The culprit in the first true story happens to be a health insurance company. An elderly woman—more than seventy-five years old, living on her own, and struggling with cancer—became overwhelmed by the number of insurance documents she was receiving on an almost daily basis. After a while, the stack of papers was so high that she gave up any hope of having the energy to get through them all. She finally called the company in the hope that someone would explain what all the papers meant and maybe make arrangements to send fewer documents. However, the representative apparently had no idea how exhausted and frightened this woman was, and his explanations were as convoluted as the insurance policy! As it turned out, when the elderly woman looked through some of the papers at random, many were not bills at all but merely itemized descriptions of services rendered. Each one stated, "No payment due."

For a company supposedly invested in a person's health, it makes little sense that its baroque bureaucratic accounting methods would "need" to be the way they are for a person who is ill, frightened, and all alone. All this woman cared about was having the strength to get up in the morning, make herself eat something, and get to her weekly chemotherapy treatments. Those who created the system and those who represent it, however, seemed unconcerned about the people they are supposed to serve. That says a lot to me about what they take to be their purpose and what values support that purpose.

The healthcare company was not the only one unwilling to keep values and purpose in mind. This same woman had put down a deposit on a carport with an Arizona-based company that delivers and installs carports all over the West and Southeast. Once they have enough orders in a region, they send out an installation crew with the carports. At the time the woman ordered the carport, the company assured her that it would be at her house within a month. It took much longer, however. She tried to cancel her order, explaining to the carport company that she was tired of waiting and wanted her deposit back. She repeatedly asked to speak with someone in a supervisory position, and when she finally succeeded, she received no satisfaction. She even went so far as to tell the supervisor that she was undergoing cancer treatment, and she didn't want to die before she got her carport. Nothing seemed to matter to this company, except that they weren't about to inconvenience themselves in order to do right by this customer. Four months after she had put down the deposit, they finally scheduled a date, which happened to coincide with her next chemotherapy appointment. Frightened that she wouldn't get her carport if she weren't home on that day, she rescheduled her chemotherapy appointment.

Any company has to reconcile the point of business—to make money—with values that may decrease profits or not thrill shareholders, and that applies to organizations with two employees or 200,000. It is imperative that you think carefully about how you can make a profit and remain true to your values. I submit that some of the companies that are considered most successful have, in reality, lost their way.

A Values and "Success" Case Study: Walmart

Consider a massively financially profitable organization like Walmart, whose corporate motto is, "Save money. Live better." Sam Walton opened the first Walmart store in Arkansas in 1962,[9] founding his company on the principle of service. "This belief that true leadership depends on willing service was the principle on which Walmart was built, and drove the decisions the company has made for the past fifty years. So much of Walmart's history is tied to the story of Sam Walton himself, and so much of our future will be rooted in Mr. Sam's princi-ples."[10] Those principles included offering quality goods at a low price and hiring employees who gave customers the sort of experience that would bring them back again and again.

Fast-forward to 2012, when you could pick up a gallon of Vlasic pickles—basically a year's supply—at Walmart for less than three bucks. It was a great buy for customers, but it arguably undermined Vlasic's standing as a premium brand.[11] And when one of the world's largest companies undercuts one of its preeminent suppliers, it's not just the customer who loses. The customer may have gained some-thing in the short term in the form of a large quantity of pickles at a cut-rate price, and Vlasic may have made a lot of sales through its arrangement with the big-box store. But what was the long-term cost? For Vlasic, it was a net loss of millions of dollars. For the customer, the cost is harder to see, but it's there, nonetheless.

Look at it this way. If Walmart's original values no longer drive the company—and I believe they do not—then the losses begin to pile up for everyone, including the consumer. Communities in close prox-imity to a Walmart lose small businesses—grocery stores, hardware stores, toy stores, electronics stores, and so forth—that cannot afford to compete with Walmart's prices. The people who run those busi-nesses are also consumers, whose purchasing power is now limited to—surprise!—what Walmart sells.

Then there are the Walmart employees—the ones Sam Walton claimed made his store a success. According to a 2007 report by Wal-Mart Watch,[12] the company faced, among other problems, "numer-ous lawsuits, including the largest gender discrimination class-action lawsuit in the nation's history."[13] In addition, the company's reputation began failing, perhaps in response to intense media scrutiny of Walmart's treatment of employees. The fact is, when companies fail to live up to the most fundamental values, such as fair treatment of employees, people notice.

Decision-Making, Values, and Emotions

It's no exaggeration to say that our values are tested every day, and that's something that may begin at a very young age. Educational psychologists have found connections between, for example, the pressure to perform on standardized tests and cheating in children as young as age seven.[14] Unfortunately, performance is increasingly valued over the process of learning.

Moreover, having an MBA or other business training won't equip you "to master the temptations, dilemmas, and tradeoffs [you're] likely to encounter."[15] Harvard business administration professor Joshua Margolis points out that there is a "responsibility gap" between what society expects from people in business and what human beings are generally capable of achieving. There seem to be "emerging responsibilities amid rapidly transforming and uncertain circumstances . . . over and above the existing financial expectations companies must meet . . . [and] mounting evidence from social science [that] reveals how limited and flawed human beings are in taking on even basic responsibilities."[16]

On one side of this gap is what Margolis calls the "emerging responsibilities." These include increased social expectations of conduct, which a business can choose to include in the scope of its existing social responsibilities. For example, historically, social support and emergency services have been the responsibility of families, communities, religious organizations, or governments. These same services are now being expected, in some fashion, of companies. That may not be a bad thing. There are times when such an organization is better equipped to do what cannot be done by a community or government. Margolis offers a stellar example. In the immediate aftermath of the 2004 tsunami in Indonesia, which killed more than 200,000 people, a small Swedish charter tour company did for tourists stranded in the area what the Swedish government failed to do:

> With little information and severed contact to the region, [Fritidsresor CEO Johan] Lundgren and his team . . . had to determine how to attend to customers and staff in the affected region, how to communicate with the public through the press, and whether to send additional planes of eager vacationers to the region, all while keeping the business operating to many other regions at the busiest time of the year . . . No one would have bet on a small, struggling tour operator with no values statement and no record of profitability to be the one to deliver during the chaos of the tsunami—certainly not if you had witnessed their emergency drill the year before. But Sweden turned its eyes to this one small company during the hours and days following the tsunami. As the government stumbled, Fritidsresor rose to the challenge, evacuating 4,500 Scandinavians from the tsunami region, whether customers or not.[17]

Where the Swedish government failed, a small company achieved extraordinary results. This is a case where the responsibility gap was actually slammed shut! Margolis's point is that there are too many people coming out of MBA and other business programs with little training in identifying, let alone bridging, this responsibility gap, especially given the fact that "ethically responsible conduct" is "not perfectly aligned" with "financial performance." Indeed, "the true challenge lies in how companies go about doing both."[18]

Yes, given increasing demands upon businesses to do and be more, it's not surprising that one might be tempted to slack off on one's values, "just this once." But I believe, and I want to convince you, that giving in to this sort of temptation will do more harm than good, both in the short and long term. It's possible to do what supports your values and achieves your purpose. We can fortify our resolve to remain committed to living out our values, especially if we take the time to prepare ourselves for the sorts of demands Margolis mentions, including demands that we cannot foresee.

Ideally, choices should not be made rashly. Few situations are as urgent as that which confronted the Swedish charter tour company in 2004. But the clearer you are about what you value, the less time you need to take making decisions when there is little time to begin with. Consider, for example, the extraordinary responses to the 2013 Boston Marathon bombings. Without knowing whether or not they were running toward danger—more bombs might have been about to explode—people rushed to the aid of those injured by the blasts. There was little deliberating about what to do and then doing it; it was a case of "just knowing" they had to help.

"Wait a minute!" you might protest. "How can we 'prepare ourselves for demands that we cannot see'?"

The short answer is simple: On an emotional level, you already know what these demands are. The vast majority of your emotional intuitions, what feels right to decide or to do, can prepare you for unforeseen demands. I'm referring to specific situations that call for you to make a decision or take some action.

Let's say that, emotionally, you want to do something, but you need to justify your actions. Sometimes, you can look at something purely rationally, but it doesn't feel right. The fact is, more than 90 percent of every decision we make is based on emotion, and more than 95 percent of our thoughts are subconscious, which drive our decisions.[19] I'm not saying you shouldn't be rational. But no matter how reasonable your decision-making was, sometimes the result is off. When I was around sixteen or seventeen years old, I remember telling my dad that I was thinking of breaking up with a girlfriend, but I was in turmoil about it. Everything indicated that she was great. Why did I want to let her go?

My dad said, "Okay, get a pad and a pen. Put a line down the middle. Put all the things about the girl on the left that you like."

So I did.

Then he said, "Now put the things you don't like on the right."

So I did.

The list on the left was longer than the list on the right.

"So," I said uncertainly, "I shouldn't break up with her, right?"

My dad said, "Wait. There's a question you have to ask yourself."

"Okay," I said, nodding. "What is it?"

"Do you love her?" He paused, then pointed at the pad of paper and said, "If not, none of the things on the left make any difference."

This story illustrates a point that Margolis thinks social scientists have established: Although we want to believe wholeheartedly in our rational ability to solve problems, the fact is we don't actually work that way. Let's apply this idea to business values. Apparently, human psychology generally falls short of the ethical demands we make on ourselves.[20] In other words, we humans don't do the best job of using our rational and emotional apparatus to its fullest extent and appropriately.[21] We reason our way through problems and weigh options, but we need emotion to make important connections meaningful.

In addition, the social scientists focusing on organizational behavior generally believe that policies generated in response to managerial wrongdoing actually perpetuate the very behaviors they are meant to curb or preclude.[22] So, let's say an investment firm has a conflict-of-interest policy, whereby all potential conflicts have to be disclosed. In those cases, the social scientists found, employees who made the disclosure "were more willing to give biased advice, and those on the receiving end did not discount the advice sufficiently."[23] It's as if the worry over appearing biased were dissolved the moment you admitted there was at least a potential for bias! Disclosure of potential bias often seems to encourage people to act on that bias.

Once we identify the ways in which human conduct doesn't always align with our ethical ideals, we are in a much better position to work out how our values can be supported in our organization. Business has always been an aspect of our daily lives, not something foreign to it. Granted, actions we would take without thinking when dealing with family and loved ones may become complicated when factors like profit need to be considered. But I believe it's pretty simple, really: You can't be two people! You can't be one person at home and another person at work. The same consideration, care, and compassion you show your loved ones at home you also bring to work.

Someone once asked me, "How are you so comfortable speaking to a room full of people?"

"I trained myself," I responded, "to speak with passion and conviction, because I pretend I'm talking to my own children. I don't condescend. I treat my audience with the concern and care I would show my family. If one of my kids was heading off into the hills on a motorcycle, I'd caution against not wearing a helmet. And just as much as I want my children to be safe and do well in their lives, I want you to be safe and do well in yours."

My value system is clear. I am a firm believer that our values are inculcated through the way we're raised, reinforced through our culture—education, community, religious beliefs, and so on—and honed by practice. You have to decide what your system is and how the parts relate to each other and work in your daily life. And as we've been discussing for several chapters now, you use them to achieve your purpose.

Apple Inc. has harnessed or created and then combined technologies and design in such a way that has utterly transformed how people live their lives. The brand has become so powerful that people continue to be loyal to Apple even when things in the relationship are less than ideal. They're willing to forgive this or that transgression because Apple is "theirs." "I'm a Mac person," is a common refrain. Apple is associated with a lifestyle; there's an Apple culture.

When you look at the history of that company, you can see how purpose, in fact, set a direction for it. Founder Steve Jobs was always pushing Apple toward innovation in technology and design. His departure in 1985 also resulted in a departure from those qualities, which had been his hallmark. His absence and subsequent return to the company in 1996 marked a recommitment to his purpose.

Without unnecessarily complicating things, it is worth pointing out that your purpose may be your organization's greatest value, or it may not. Remember Dennis Mehiel, CEO of U.S. Display Group and a longtime corrugated-box-manufacturing expert? The purpose of his company, from the standpoint of function, is to make good quality point-of-purchase displays. The purpose of U.S. Display Group, from the standpoint of stated corporate goals, is "to be an asset for our customers through the products and services that we provide."[24] The company's values direct conduct in ways that can be both integral to its purpose and independent of it. The goal of being an asset to customers is achieved through the value of producing quality products and quality services.[25] In this case, purpose and value go hand-in-hand. Another value is the organization's "commitment to environmental and social responsibility." This value appears to be independent of, but still complementary to U.S. Display Group's purpose. Knowing this distinction will help you think more clearly about what you value and how it is related to what you do. Ask yourself, "What is my organization's purpose?" and "How are my values integrated with it or operating independently of it?"

TOMS is in the business of selling specialized types of shoes and sunglasses. The functional purpose is clear. The goal, on the other hand, is a value: "We are in business to help change lives."[26] For every pair of shoes purchased, a pair of shoes is donated to a child in need. Similarly, for every pair of sunglasses purchased, some sight care is provided, be it a pair of glasses, a contribution toward eye surgery, or medical treatment. It's called One for One™. There is no immediate connection between the functional purpose of the company—manufacturing and selling shoes and sunglasses—and the company's values. They can be disconnected from each other. To the extent, however, that TOMS founder Blake Mycoskie envisioned consumers as benefactors, value was built into the company's final purpose.

Another way you can begin to think about the relation between your organization's purpose, values, and activities is to create a grid that lays out each of these areas. It could look something like one of these:

Chipotle Mexican Grill		
Value	Purpose	Action
Environmentally Sustainable Food Production	Create affordable, quickly prepared food from the finest ingredients	Partner with farmers and ranchers committed to sustainable food production
Ethical Food Production	Create affordable, quickly prepared food from the finest ingredients	Partner with farmers and ranchers committed to ethical food production

U.S. Display Group

Value	Purpose	Purpose	Action
Quality products	Produce quality point-of-purchase displays	"to be an asset for our customers through the products and services that we provide"	Hire the best talent (and be willing to pay for it) and implement the best processes.
Commitment to environmental and social responsibility	Produce quality point-of-purchase displays		Use recycled cardboard

TOMS

Value	Purpose	Purpose	Action
Quality, environmentally sustainable products	Take care of our resources		Offer shoes with sustainable & vegan materials
Corporate responsibility	Take care of our resources	Offer as many people as possible footwear & eyewear/eyecare	Offer shoes with sustainable & vegan materials One for One
Improving people's lives	Offer as many people as possible footwear & eyewear/eyecare		One for One

The next step to acting on your values and purposes, of course, is to promote it by getting those outside the organization on board and involved. That is the subject of our next few chapters.

CHAPTER 11

THE HEART OF GETTING OTHERS INVOLVED IN YOUR PURPOSE

WHEN YOU DO NOTHING YOU FEEL OVERWHELMED AND
POWERLESS. BUT WHEN YOU GET INVOLVED YOU FEEL THE
SENSE OF HOPE AND ACCOMPLISHMENT THAT COMES FROM
KNOWING YOU ARE WORKING TO MAKE THINGS BETTER.
—MAYA ANGELOU

Let's suppose human beings believe purposeful actions are meaningful. It's a reasonable idea. After all, people write, create art, undertake home improvement projects, and exercise or participate in sports. Perhaps most importantly, people do not engage in activities they don't believe are meaningful in some way. Why do people respond to a cry for help from another person? They do it because they believe the action will be helpful: that, as Maya Angelou tells us, the action will contribute to "making things better." And they want to do it because something in them tells them it's a good thing to do. This belief in the meaningfulness of certain actions seems to be a crucial feature of how we make decisions.

It's a Jungle Out There

Unfortunately, these days, it's easy to feel despondent and helpless. How can we feel that we're making things better when there is just so much that's going wrong? How can we even know what to do when everything seems equally urgent? Information comes at us 24/7 in astonishingly large batches from a variety of sources: e-mail; Web sites; cable or satellite television; phone; texts. The information is buzzing and fuzzy, and things get jumbled together into an indiscernible blob.

There's so much going on that it's nearly impossible to achieve a concentrated focus on one topic unless it's catastrophic or ridiculous enough to cut through the noise. Even then, the world keeps spinning fast, and the instant news cycle means stories don't live very long. How do we keep up? And even if we can keep up, how do we feel anything but overwhelmed and helpless to do anything meaningful? There are so many causes, needs, and urgent requests out there that you can get dizzy just thinking about them. How can we choose which need or cause or emergency is most important?

Decision Fatigue

The situation reminds me of several interesting studies on how our environment affects our ability to choose. The first involves "decision fatigue." "No matter how rational and high-minded you try to be, you can't make decision after decision without paying a biological price."[1] That price is fatigue. According to one study, judges presiding over multiple parole hearings in a single day became tired, and their decisions reflect that. "Prisoners who appeared early in the morning received parole about 70 percent of the time, while those who appeared late in the day were paroled less than 10 percent of the time."[2] The researchers concluded that "judicial rulings can be swayed by extraneous variables that should have no bearing on legal decisions."[3]

A similar conclusion was reached in an earlier study about consumer choices. Where we typically think that the more choices we get to make, the better off we are—that more options somehow equate to greater freedom—this study shows that it can actually drain our physical resources. "Making choices led to reduced self-control (that is, less physical stamina, [less] task persistence in the fact of failure, more procrastination, and less quality and quantity of arithmetic calculations.)"[4] This consequence is related to the number of choices offered: We're less likely to make a choice because we feel paralyzed. Two other responses to the same situation are poor choice or dissatisfaction with the choice after the fact.[5] Maybe that's why Albert Einstein owned multiple versions of one outfit. One less choice to make every day—even on something as trivial as what to wear—means more energy spent on things like revolutionary work in physics!

Still another study focuses on poverty and short-term decision-making. We already know that studies have shown that, in some cases, the more choices people are offered, the harder it is for people to make a decision. Imagine you are so poor you cannot simply go into the store and buy what you want. Necessities such as toothpaste, toilet paper, soap, and so forth have to be weighed carefully in terms of price and urgency. So whereas you or I probably walk into a store looking for our favorite brand and type of toothpaste with no need to think about competing brands and types, a poor person has to compare prices. Now imagine doing this over and over throughout the day, every day. The sheer volume of minute choices that have to be made leaves one utterly exhausted.[6]

Despite the breakneck rate of speed at which life is lived today, and despite the extraordinary number of distractions from what's really important, it is still possible for people to discern something authentic. In fact, people actually crave authenticity as an inoculation against, or antidote to the chaotic buzz of superficiality and crassness that typifies the types of shocking behaviors displayed in, for example, the financial services industry scandals. They search for companies that provide them with a meaningful customer experience.

What Is a Meaningful Experience?

According to a 2012 survey conducted by The Values Institute,[7] "today's most trustworthy brands have created relationships with consumers through experiences that trigger a visceral response."[8] But what, exactly, does that mean? Evidently, according to an article in *Entrepreneur* magazine, the "Top Ten" experiences are characterized by the following slogans and their brands:[9]

1. Get personal (Amazon)

2. Sell happiness (Coca-Cola)

3. Live up to your promise (FedEx)

4. Keep it cool (and fun; Apple)

5. Design an experience (Target)

6. Stay consistent (Ford)

7. Can-do attitude (Nike)

8. Forge connections (Starbucks)

9. Serve up the quirky (Southwest Airlines)

10. Focus on the customer (Nordstrom)

Each one of these approaches to branding is claimed to create an emotional response and therefore a connection that, in turn, creates loyalty. But some of the items on the list are vague. Just what is happiness, anyway? And I'm not convinced that all of them really exemplify a visceral response or something truly authentic. Let's look at each one in detail.

AMAZON

Lots of online companies have folded, so there is no question that Amazon is doing something right. But is its success really due to the fact that it's "personal"? Online experiences are always personal, or at least intimate. When you sit down in front of the screen, just as when you sit down with a book, you are not interacting with another physical person. You are having internal interactions. It's similar to what happens when you read a book. You enter another world, to be sure, but it's lived in your mind. So, it seems to me that Amazon must be doing something in addition to "making it personal."

COCA-COLA

The famous soda is consistently darn tasty, no doubt about it. It's also been around long enough to become iconic; it has been a part of so many important events in people's lives that it's almost a family member. The marketing genius behind the brand is that happiness, so difficult to define, yet yearned for by so many, feels tangible to each of us. In other words, we import our own definition of happiness onto the product, and then associate that product with that happiness. Clever.

FEDEX

Delivering on your promise time and again is fundamental to creating the sort of emotional response in customers that makes a brand a brand.[10] In fact, living up to your promise is exactly what we expect from people who want our trust, and it's what we expect from ourselves when we want people to trust us!

APPLE

There is no question that Apple's cool factor works. But if we ask what's so cool about Apple, we're told that the products "improve the way [we] communicate." Sure, the purchase experience is said to be fun, but when you're spending the sort of money commanded by an Apple product, fun is not really the issue.

TARGET

My bone of contention with the "design an experience" idea is similar to the "cool factor" attributed to Apple. Target has developed from discount store to stylish discount store by focusing on design. But stylishness is meaningless if there is no substance to back it up, as we'll discover in a later chapter. No hip design can overcome products that look great but don't function well or last long. Fortunately for Target, it appears that with more stylish design has also come a better quality product. Target's transformation is a corporate version of the American dream: from humble beginnings can emerge stylishly spectacular success.

FORD

Consistency of quality, which translates to trustworthiness, is another real value. Ford is associating itself with American ideals of solid, straightforward, and pragmatic products.

NIKE

Nike's optimism is expressed in the can-do (or "just do it") attitude. This is another quintessentially American value, and so it resonates with our inborn aspirations.

STARBUCKS

Bringing people together over a cup of coffee seems like a no-brainer. But no one has been as astronomically successful at setting the conditions for forging connections as Starbucks. After the novelty of café lattés and decaf-chai-mocha-no-whip-with-skim-milk drinks—and the price tags that went with them—wore off, Starbucks could have taken a nosedive. Instead, they're more ubiquitous nationwide than McDonald's! Why? According to Howard Schultz, Starbucks CEO, "If people relate to the company they work for, if they form an emotional tie to it and buy into its dreams, they will pour their heart into making it better."[11]

For Schulz, the Starbucks experience is not just about a meeting place, although large tables and comfortable chairs are certainly conducive to it. It's also a place where the employees know their regulars and their orders before the customer walks in the door. That's what makes Starbucks stand apart.

SOUTHWEST

I don't think "serving up the quirky" is why people fly Southwest. Sure, it's fun to hear flight attendants sing the safety instructions. But take it from someone who travels a lot: singing doesn't cut it, especially in the flying-bus era of air travel. What underlies Southwest's success is the same sort of consistency and delivery of a promise that make Ford and FedEx successful. These are core values that emphasize an authentic customer experience. Gimmicks, almost by definition, never last.

NORDSTROM

"When mythic stories circulate about your company's awesome customer service, you know you're doing something right. That's the hallmark of this upscale department store, which is rumored to have once graciously accepted the return of a set of tires, even though the store has never sold tires."[12] Yup, that pretty much says everything you need to know about Nordstrom's commitment to exceptional customer service. Its business is different from, say, FedEx, but the value of living up to your promise stands out here, and it's the main reason Nordstrom remains a high-end yet widely respected brand. The company somehow manages to eschew elitism in its approach to customer service, while remaining an elite brand in the public consciousness.

People Get Involved in What Matters to Them: The Emotional Core of Values

Despite the fact that we live in a world full of a dizzying array of products, services, offerings, wants, needs, problems, and solutions, if you can clearly articulate your values and identify your purpose, you are going to be able to determine what is important to you. As we've seen, the challenge is getting others to want to realize your purpose with you. My solution is simple. You need to make your purpose both personally meaningful and authentic.

Whether you are in a leadership position, want to be in a leadership position, or are interested in the connection between values and business, moving forward toward your goals requires that you have a crystal-clear vision of what's important. Remember the elderly woman I told you about in chapter 10—the one who was utterly overwhelmed by the insurance paperwork piling up on her desk when she should have been focusing on her cancer treatment? Just imagine that you are the person responsible for the way the insurance company organizes its tracking system, or that you're responsible for how representatives help insured patients navigate their policy. Would you think you'd done a good job if you were responsible for what this woman experienced? I hope the answer is no.

This is not about thinking how you'd feel if this woman were your mother or grandmother. It's about understanding how to treat people with respect, no matter who they are. Real leaders recognize this value as fundamental to all human interactions. I believe that respect involves empathy.

Empathy Is Our Genetic Inheritance

You can read hundreds upon hundreds of marketing books, advertising how-to's, articles on selling strategies and techniques, and tomes on speaking and communicating. How do you know which approach works best? My standard answer to that question—which, believe me, I get asked all the time—is this: You must appeal to your audience's emotions. It's that simple. People don't choose rationally to listen to your message and then have a feeling about it. They choose to listen to your message because they have a feeling about it. All the content, process, features, and benefits in the world will matter little to another individual if that information is not connecting on a relevant, meaningful, and emotional level.

We've talked a lot about values already in this book, but I'm going to take a bit of time here to argue for the view that our values have an emotional core. Bear with me.

There has been interesting scientific research about the origin of morality. For almost a half-century, biologist and primatologist Frans de Waal has studied human beings' closest relatives, chimpanzees and bonobos, which share "almost 99 percent of the human genome."[13] De Waal has focused much of his recent research on the origins of morality: that system of values and principles of conduct that guide our distinctions between right and wrong and good and bad actions.

According to de Waal,[14] morality is a product of evolution, not a product of learning or choice, and his research has documented behaviors interpreted as sharing, cooperating, and empathizing. In one study, for example, chimps were allowed to choose between two tokens, one that would yield a food reward only for the chooser, and one that would yield a food reward for the chooser and an observer. The study found that chimps almost always chose the token that yielded the reward for both the chooser and observer. This behavior is considered empathy-based altruism.[15] So, the question is: Are there baseline values that are hardwired into our systems? In other words, if chimps are humans' closest genetic relatives, and if chimps appear to have a biological disposition toward empathy, does that mean human beings are naturally empathic, too? That would give us a foundation for a host of values, such as fairness and reciprocity.

Perhaps, as de Waal points out, traits like empathy are a sort of sensitivity and responsiveness to others' feelings. When you see

someone sad, you're sad for them and with them. When you see someone happy, you're happy for them and with them. If someone looks
lonely, you wish they had a friend. You get the idea.

What I think is useful about a discussion of de Waal's work in the
context of this chapter is that people resonate with each other at a
deep, biological level. When I say that research has shown more than
90 percent of our decisions are driven by emotion, I'm saying that
there are some basic, biological aspects to the values that characterize
human beings' interactions with each other.

One more thing . . . Extraordinary advances in technology have
allowed neuroscientists to learn more about the brain in the past fifteen
years than in the past 150. We now know, for example, that our limbic
system regulates emotion and memory. The right temporal parietal junc-
tion of the brain is that tiny part above the right ear that wonders what
other people are thinking. These biological functions are not immediately
related to values, but they make them possible; they're a foundation.

In my presentations about branding through emotional connections, I tell people that we need to expand the idea of how the brain
thinks about thinking and connect it to the function of the limbic
system. We need to figure out what people would love and what they
truly desire! That's because, if I am correct about our values having an
emotional or biological core, then the more we understand about how
our brains work, the more likely it is that we will succeed in making
meaningful connections with others.

Empathy Does Not Mean We All Think the Same Way

Your concept of fairness may diverge considerably from that of your
neighbor. But the fact that you and your neighbor both still believe
in fairness as a value, and the fact that you come across others whose

values correlate with yours, suggests to me that there are common baseline values that spring from the same source.[16]

If these values are truly part of who we are, then incorporating them into our projects and organizations is pretty much a no-brainer. According to a panel of leaders convened by *Forbes*, for example, empathy is essential to both successful leadership and the concept of business.[17] How empathy manifests in specific instances, however, may vary. One parent may choose to type up their child's essay because they see the child struggling with how to develop an idea; another may refuse to do so because they want the child to learn how to cope with struggles.

If you agree that empathy can and does show itself in different guises, I am confident you'll be in a much better position to articulate your own values and purpose, to surround yourself with people who share them, to be open to communicating with those whose values and purpose may differ from yours, and to get others excited about your project or organization.

An Emotional Branding and Values Case Study: Patagonia

Patagonia, originally known as Chouinard Equipment, is the outdoor clothing and gear company founded in the late 1950s by Yvon Chouinard, a guy who fell in love with rock climbing and the outdoor life. He wanted to create reusable pitons, the spikes driven into rock or cracks in rock to support climbers.[18] At the time, pitons were left behind after a climb, littering majestic mountain rock faces. When Chouinard came up with an alternative, his pitons were a big success, and he made a living traveling up and down the California coast forging and selling his wares. Some great surfing and other mountain climbing gear was thrown into the mix for good measure.

By 1970, however, Chouinard realized the piton business was environmentally unsustainable. "Climbing had become more popular, but remained concentrated on the same well-tried routes . . . The same fragile cracks had to endure repeated hammering of pitons, during both placement and removal, and the disfiguring was severe."[19] Despite the fact that his company was the largest manufacturer of pitons in the United States, Chouinard could not reconcile his love of the outdoors with the damage pitons were doing to once-pristine rock faces. Fortunately, a more environmentally friendly aluminum chock was developed, and climbing became "clean." So began what would become a foundational brick in Patagonia's environmentalism. CEO Casey Sheahan said it best: "Our company is almost masquerading as an apparel manufacturer. We're really more concerned with protecting the planet."[20]

It's not easy to be environmentally conscientious, but the commitment to what has increasingly been called a social justice issue is non-negotiable for this outdoor wear and gear company. "Once you start," it says on the company Web page, "you can't stop."[21]

Patagonia is an example of what has been called values-driven ventures.[22] These have typically been associated with social responsibility. For example, a nonprofit organization may have as its mission ensuring that all people have access to clean water by installing water filtration systems in underdeveloped countries. But for-profit businesses may also emotionally connect with people—and get them on board with their purpose—on the basis of their values, as we'll see in the following chapter.

CHAPTER 12

GOOD, BETTER, AND BEST WAYS TO GET OTHERS ON BOARD TO ACHIEVE YOUR PURPOSE

*IT'S VERY DIFFICULT TO GET THE RIGHT PEOPLE WHO
HAVE THE SAME PASSION INTO THE PATH AND ACTUALLY LIVE
IT. BUT WHEN YOU GET IT THEN YOU KNOW YOU GOT IT
BECAUSE THEY LIVE ON WHAT YOU WANT.*

—EMMA KIMANI

I believe two kinds of people are most likely to jump on board and get involved with your organization. First are those who are already interested in the values and purpose reflected in your activities. Second, where those values are not immediately reflected in your activities, are those people who understand and believe in your purpose. Let's look at some examples of each to get a better idea of what I mean.

Values-Driven Activities: Good, Better, and Best Approaches to Getting People on Board

Let's focus for a moment on some of the more obvious types of val-ue-laden activities, such as veterans' aid and support organizations, childhood disease research institutions, poverty eradication nonprof-its, educational opportunities, and animal welfare groups. The people working on these issues are doing things they believe in. You may actually think they're all equally worthy of attention. So if someone is trying to get you on board, how would you decide?

You'd probably look for more specificity in the way the activity is described so that you could better determine whether or not the organization's activities reflect your own priorities, time, and available resources. Suppose you had always valued service to one's country and were outraged by the stories that began to circulate around 2004 about service members who lost their place at school, their job, or their houses because they had to ship off to war for a tour of duty. You could look for nonprofit organizations that focused on educa-tional and employment services for military veterans, especially those who have served in Iraq and Afghanistan.[1] You conclude that you have the time and money to make a difference. However, you still want to weigh other options.

Suppose you also valued rescuing stray dogs and were dismayed to hear about the increasing number of animals abandoned after the economy crashed. There are myriad rescue organizations that place shelter dogs and cats in foster homes, and it's something you'd like to do. Unfortunately, you don't have the space to be a foster volunteer, and it just feels more urgent for you to work on the veterans' cause. There: you've made your choice.

Let's take a closer look at how you arrived at your conclusion. I believe you made your decision by reflecting and understanding what you value and assessing the presentation of each organization; in other words, it was through an emotional, relevant, and visceral connection backed by rationality.

GOOD, BUT NOT GREAT—IT'S ONLY ONE PART OF THE SOLUTION

One approach to getting people to engage with your ideas is to focus on presentation.[2] This means using rhetorical devices to connect with people who are already committed to the same values as yours. An example is a three-step method to organizing your presentation: context, framing, and content.

Setting the context and providing a framework for your idea helps people to quickly understand the situation and what you're trying to do; there's no guesswork. And once your audience is receptive to the idea, they'll be less likely to reject the content. This is merely part of the overall process, but unfortunately for many people, this is where they stop. Too many people and too many organizations believe presentation—essentially, marketing, without a commitment to purpose—is the magic bullet, and they don't think beyond it.

I tried this approach once, years ago, when I was still fairly new to the advertising and marketing business. I was clueless about the emotional component of the selling process. I had a client in North Carolina, a distributor who had contractors throughout the state. These contractors were indirectly my clients, too, since they were benefiting from their distributor. The distributor also had sales reps, also known as territory managers, who were responsible for selling to these contractors. Our agency had developed a truly wonderful program meant to immediately increase sales for the contractors, which would in turn increase sales for the distributor. Greater sales for the contractors also meant more commission for the territory managers. I thought that would be obvious to these guys. I was wrong.

When I went to their offices to make a presentation, I asked Ernie, the vice president of sales and the point person for the client, to make sure his territory managers were in the room. I proceeded to lay out the start dates, costs, media coverage, print ads, radio and television commercials, and the desired and expected outcomes. In other words, I explained all the features and benefits. I then told the territory managers that the agency had produced packets for them to bring to their contractors to help explain the program.

After I'd finished, one of the territory managers said, "Scott, this is your program and your campaign, not mine. Promoting this campaign isn't my responsibility. I'm responsible for selling product to these guys. I don't see anywhere in my employee contract where I'm supposed to help our advertising agency sell their programs. I'm not interested."

Every other territory manager voiced the same comments. They understood what I was doing and why, but it just didn't resonate with them. Now I could have simply told the client to demand these guys get on board. After all, they were employees of the company, and I was its contracted advertising agency. Believe me, that's exactly what I wanted to do. Fortunately, as we'll see shortly, my client stopped me.

I'm not saying the context, framing, and content strategy isn't a good approach for presenting your ideas. Actually, it's imperative. What I am saying is that it does not provide a complete picture of what successfully results in getting people to sign on to your project or organization's purpose. Neither does touting the perks of the job, whether it's "Flexible Fridays," employee ownership options, or awards for good work. Again, it's not that these aren't good things; they are. It's just that they're not enough to achieve and sustain the level of commitment you want for your organization. We're talking about features and benefits, policies and procedures, price and content versus meaningful, relevant, and visceral connections.

You may have heard the saying, "They're buying you." I don't accept that as the whole story! It's not sufficient to get people to "buy you."[3] I don't agree, moreover, that, "what really matters most in business is how well you do in getting others to like you, trust you, and believe in you."[4] I have no doubt it is imperative that people trust you. I also have no doubt it is really good if people like you. Finally, I have no doubt that part of what people do when they commit to your project or organization is that they buy you. Ultimately, however, they're buying the values and purpose you've established, and they're buying what's important to them. Insofar as you embody those values and purpose, it's reasonable to say that people who sign on to your project or organization are buying you.

BETTER, BUT STILL NOT GREAT

Another approach to getting people on board is to find out what others want, whether they're employees, volunteers, or customers.[5] Finding and keeping employees who are engaged with their jobs and want to come to work every day is no easy task. Understanding their needs goes partway to making a lasting connection with them. The problem is that you're going in the wrong direction.

Of course, you should care about what the people in your organization want and need, and, in fact, this is a value. But the focus here should be on your clear and demonstrated commitment to your values and purpose, which will pique the interest of those who share them. If you don't already have your own values and purpose worked out and you try to derive them survey-style, you'll forever be at the beck and call of differing people's needs and wants.

WE HAVE A WINNER! BEST APPROACHES TO GETTING OTHERS ON BOARD AND INVOLVED

One way of looking at the balance you want to strike is in terms of authenticity.[6] An authentic organization, according to business researcher, educator, and speaker CV Harquail, is one whose members continuously work at aligning the organization's identity, image, and actions. I take that to be consistent with my idea of clearly articulating a purpose, which is realized through exercising values every day. The only way that happens is if the individuals who make up the organization have a shared commitment to that purpose and those values.

Let me tell you the rest of the story about my presentation to the distributor's sales reps. After I failed to get the territory managers on board with our program, one of them asked Ernie, my contact, "Is that it? Can we go?"

After they left the room, I looked at Ernie helplessly and said, "We've known each other for several years now, and we have a great relationship. Yes, we love hanging out, we golf, and we tell great jokes at dinner, but if that's all I brought to this relationship, I would ask you to fire me today."

Ernie looked at me patiently and waited for me to continue.

"We have helped your company grow," I went on, "and we've

helped your contractors reach new business heights. I know this program will work, but these guys need to be on board. They work for you, right? Why don't you demand they present and promote the program to their contractors?"

Ernie heard me out and said, "Tell you what. I'll bring them back into the room, but you need to tell them, not me."

In that moment, I knew he was right. I knew I needed to say to that group of guys what I had said to Ernie, and they needed to see my commitment.

So back into the room they came. The ringleader, apparently put out at having to return, said, "What's up? I thought we were done."

I stood up. "I know. But listen, guys. I want to ask each of you a question, and I want your honest answer. Do you care about your customers on a personal level? Is it important to you that they succeed?"

Each one responded with comments like, "Of course, we care about them," and, "Yes, we want them to succeed."

"Okay, good, because that's essential," I continued.

I got a few bored stares. They didn't know where this was going and didn't seem particularly interested. But my next question got their attention. "Do you love your families? Do you want to provide for them in a way that they'll never have to worry about financial problems, vacations, or college?"

Again, the responses were, "Well, of course," and, "You know we do."

Some of the guys started sitting up a bit straighter, paying a little more attention. "Where are you going with this kind of questioning?" one of them asked.

I held up the program packet again and said, "This program will immediately improve your contractors'—your customers'—sales and their quality of life. And they will love you for it. Why? Because you will be the one to bring it to them, you will become their hero. You will become irreplaceable. And, when they start making more money because of this program, the very program that you will present to them, you will start making more money. That means a better quality of life for you and your family."

Little lightbulbs were going off above heads all over the room. The tension eased, replaced with a sense of excitement.

"Gentlemen, I am not trying to sell you something because I want more business, and I'm not asking you to do my job. The simple fact of the matter is this is an amazing growth opportunity for all of us. Now, are you in, or are you out?"

They looked at each other and then at the ringleader. "We're in, Scott," they said. "When you put it that way, we're in."

It was then that I realized the true difference between selling stuff and selling purpose. I had told these sales reps everything about the promotion except the most important part: what it would mean to them, what they valued, and how it would help them achieve their purpose.

I had a similar experience a number of years later when I was trying to get sixty people at my agency involved in a children's diabetes fundraising campaign. My first thought was to use the context-framing-content approach—not because I didn't know the difference by then, but because I really didn't have the time—or so I thought—to put much more into the project. I also realized that although these people were my employees, they were not obligated to do something on their own time. Like everyone else, these folks were understandably busy with other things in their lives. So I went with context, framing, and content, and the results were the same as the story above. No interest. But this was a very important cause to me, and I knew these were good people who would get interested if it became personal and important to them, too. So I put in a call to Julie.

Julie was the mother of a diabetic child, a boy named Tommy who was around seven years old at the time. He was a classmate and friend of our daughter Nicole. Julie came to the conference room where I had assembled my staff. With her was all the paraphernalia she had to carry around with her to make sure her son was safe. Nervously, she began describing the process she went through every day, beginning first thing in the morning. As she began to talk, she looked at her son and began to cry. Tommy just stared at her.

When she gathered her composure, she went on to describe how difficult it was to constantly tell a young, rambunctious boy that he could not do this or could not eat that. You could see how frazzled she was from the constant worry that her son could go into a diabetic coma if his blood sugar was dangerously abnormal. It soon became clear that this woman's entire life revolved around her child's illness, not the joys we normally think of when we consider our own children. As I looked around the room, I was touched by what I saw. All the people in the room, even the macho guys, were wiping tears from their face. At that moment, everyone there was ready to work on the campaign.

Perhaps no one is better at genuinely connecting with people than my wife, Deborah. Always volunteering or organizing charitable events, she is a master at knowing how to get the best out of the people around her. Since our granddaughter, Amaya, died, Deborah has worked tirelessly on behalf of home safety issues, especially for low-income or underprepared parents. Most often, these folks want to do the best they can for their children, but they either don't know how or can't afford the sort of safety measures that many of us take for granted.

When Deb organized the 2013 Safe and Sound with Amaya event—the First Annual Butterfly Release—she connected with each individual on an emotional level. If she needed someone to man one of the many hamburger grills for the food court, she appealed to a person's culinary skills. She got people on board and involved because they believed the purpose was noble and because they knew they could help in a meaningful way. That's how she enlisted police, fire, ambulance, and other emergency workers to volunteer their time on a hot Sunday afternoon. They showed up in uniform ready to staff the booths that served as checkpoints in the park where the event was held. The idea was that each family member would get a "passport" that was stamped at every learning station. When they completed their tour, they could turn in their passport at the entrance of the pavilion in exchange for some fun gifts and rewards for their participation. They then went inside to eat, drink, and mingle with the other families.

At the end of the event, each person was given a small box, along with instructions to hold out the box and, on the count of three, open the lid. All at once, butterflies filled the park. Deb had arranged for a shipment of dormant butterflies that slowly awakened, ready to fly off when released.

It was a magical day, and even before it was over, volunteers were asking about the next year's event and how they could be part of the steering committee. Because Deb understood that people need to connect with activities they find meaningful, she was able to get lots of different people involved.

Why These Are the Winning Approaches

A crucial segment of my corporate presentations involves a video.[7] It's a version of a story that has been around for a while, but it shows us the power of making connections to the feelings that drive our values. In the video, a blind man sits next to a sign that reads, "I'm blind. Please help." People walk by. A few drop coins in his direction; most ignore him.

At one point, a woman walks up and studies the sign. She picks it up, pulls a marker out from her coat pocket, and writes something on the card. As she writes, the man touches her shoes, as if to identify her. She then puts the sign down and walks away. Shortly thereafter, the money starts pouring in.

Later, the woman reappears, and the man touches her shoes and, realizing who she is, asks her what she did. "I wrote the same, but in different words," she says. We then see the sign, which now reads, "It's a beautiful day, and I can't see it."

You can't get people to listen to you until they feel a connection with what you want to say. "I'm Blind" does not resonate because we simply cannot relate or begin to understand what that must be like. "It's a beautiful day, and I can't see it" hits us hard because we can relate.

When people unite around shared values, and these values are lived through the organization's activities, the probability that organization will benefit at the expense of others is pretty low, and people recognize that. Of course, embracing values comes with responsibility, and even when a business does not seek out such responsibility, society increasingly demands it. As a 2011 Harvard Business Review essay points out, "the more business has begun to embrace social responsibility, the more it has been blamed for society's failures."[8] The consequence, according to the article, is increased scrutiny and legislation, which work against competition and growth.

The Harvard authors' solution is for companies to "create shared values," widening the conceptual scope of capitalism. "The purpose of the corporation must be redefined as creating shared value, not just profit per se."[9]

The Harvard essay dismisses the notion that economic success and social benefit are mutually exclusive, but it also claims that if you want to do some social good, you have to suffer a profit loss. The examples they use are helpful: Fulfilling safety requirements and hiring the disabled are socially good things, but they cost money to implement. Consequently, the company's profits are reduced.

It seems to me that the model described—which unfortunately fits a large number of organizations—reflects a disconnect between values and purpose. And it doesn't address the importance of seeing a difference between a liability and an opportunity. At the very least, it seems shortsighted for a company to resist improvements or accommodations that can actually contribute to increased productivity, for example, or innovations that come from having to re-conceptualize the workplace and individual workflow.

It's useful to recall Chipotle founder Steve Ells, who wanted to start a restaurant chain that offered tasty, healthy, ethically produced, and affordable food. Yes, he had to solve a problem: how to provide copious quantities of food without resorting to industrial farmers. Instead of compromising his values or seeing an obstacle, however, Ells saw an opportunity for a relationship with a certain type of farmer and rancher who could provide him with what he needed. They, in turn, would be able to grow with the business. Shared values led to economic success.

Pulling It All Together

People resonate emotionally with certain causes, activities, and goals, and you can tap into that emotional connection by making sure that you've clearly and carefully identified your purpose and your values and, wherever possible, you've aligned them. If that's not possible, you can nevertheless articulate how they are connected, so that all facets and levels of your organization have coherent values. You'll end up with something like the values and purpose grid I created in chapter 11. Doing so will help you see how certain activities are both crucial to your business and your values, and whether or not they align directly with your organization's purpose.

Ultimately, getting people excited about what you're doing means living a culture of values that others can see themselves living. They can see themselves in the values you've articulated. Nothing is more compelling than that!

CHAPTER 13

TO PROMOTE YOUR PURPOSE, CREATE INTRIGUE

I BELIEVE IT IS THE QUALITY OF THE RELATIONSHIPS AND

YOUR ABILITY TO MAKE AUTHENTIC CONNECTIONS THAT MOST

GREATLY IMPACTS YOUR TRUE WORTH.

—PORTER GALE

The room was stark. Bare, concrete walls were painted a drab gray. Scuffmarks marred the linoleum floor. Tinny sounds echoed sharply off every surface, exaggerating the feeling of being enclosed. Before me sat about thirty young men—some boys, actually—ranging in age from sixteen to eighteen. They all wore jumpsuits the same drab color as the walls. In fact, the young men were the only things in the room that weren't drab. These guys were restless, suspicious, scared, angry, and confused; for some of them, all these feelings were rolled into one. They were sitting there because they had to. It was evening at a New York county jail. These kids had nowhere else to go.

Several of them would be heading to the penitentiary when they came of age. Others would be released from this facility in less than a year. From the looks of them, I wouldn't be surprised if they were back. Recidivism is rampant in places like this. It's hard to pinpoint a single cause for that when there are so many to choose from: drugs; shattered home life; poverty; no education; no real community; no hope for a better future; no feeling of purpose. When the causes converge, it's a recipe for disaster. How in the world does someone like me connect with these kids?

I'd spoken to incarcerated young men before. The experience was both gratifying and eye-opening, and I knew that I'd have to stretch to meet them. They weren't interested in meeting me at all, let alone halfway.

Some of the guys were slumped in their metal chairs, staring into space. A few were busy checking their fingernails or comparing tattoos. Luckily for me, one guy had a deck of cards.

"Do me a favor?" I asked the kid with the cards.

He frowned at me. He wasn't used to being asked favors, at least not from someone like me.

"Pass the deck to the guy next to you," I said, "and tell him to shuffle the cards." Then I addressed the whole group. "I want to try a card trick with you."

The room quieted down a bit.

"This guy," I said pointing to the one with the deck, "is going to pick a card from the deck and then put it back. Then I'm going to ask a few of you to shuffle the deck. Then I'm going to pick out the card this guy chose."

A bunch of them laughed derisively. A few hands waved me off. Some used colorful language for 'No way, man.'

"It's okay. It's okay," I said smiling. "I know you don't believe me. But you will!"

The kid pulled out his card, studied it, showed it to the guys around him, and then put it back in the deck. A few guys took turns shuffling the deck. Then they passed it up to me.

I pulled out the queen of hearts. "Is this your card?" I asked.

The room was suddenly roaring with hoots and laughter and surprise. And that's when I knew we had connected.

Once everyone had quieted down, I told them I had a story I wanted to share with them. They listened with rapt attention as I told them about the day Amaya had died, and how it had impacted so many people. I told them I worried about their little brothers and little sisters, and that, whether they were outside or serving time, they could do things to change lives. I challenged them to truly examine their choices, understand the long-term consequences, and realize that there is no way they can do the wrong thing and end up in the right place.

"Just like the harm and death caused in senseless crime is preventable," I told them, "so is the harm and death caused by the simple lack of a safety strap."

What it took for me to engage with this group was not a trick but an opportunity for them to see me as someone they wanted to listen to. And as any good leader knows, people will listen to you if they know you genuinely want to listen to them, not merely lecture or talk. The intrigue that captures their attention can't be better than the product or story that it's wrapped around. The substance has to follow for the intrigue to make sense. And the substance of what you deliver should be intimately connected to your values.

When I ran my own agency, I knew that intrigue was crucial to getting a potential client involved, but if I failed to deliver something of substance, I'd never had secured those clients, or I'd have soon lost them. And the key to delivering substance was research.

Every time we pitched a company, we made bold claims, but they were always backed up by facts. The formula was simple enough: Ask the right question about the organization, provide an answer, and then provide a solution. Let me explain. Okidata was a company we wanted badly because we knew they were in a great position. They had a great product and great engineering. They were one of the pioneers of color-printing technology but then sold that technology to other printing companies like Lexmark and HP, because they were focused at the time on black-and-white and dot-matrix/impact printing. Armed with the new technology, however, Okidata's competitors were taking off. Okidata soon recognized that they were missing a very good opportunity—one they had helped create. In short, Okidata had everything going for them except they weren't making a dent in the market that they helped give birth to! By doing extensive research, we'd identified a problem, and then we came up with a solution. The intrigue we created was simply designed to get them to the table to talk with us about how we could help.

We built a box that looked sort of like a Rubik's cube, but every time you moved a part of it, a message would appear. The first message was a question: Who helped create color-printing technology? The second message was an answer: Okidata. The third message was another question: Who owns the color-printing market? The fourth message was another answer: Not Okidata! The fifth message was yet another question: Would you like to be a REAL player in the color-printing market? Then, the final message revealed the payoff: WE CAN HELP!

We sent the box with a letter to Okidata's vice president of sales and marketing. Not fifteen minutes after she opened the package, she called our director. "How do you know this?" She asked. Then she added, "And how fast can you get here?"

We went with a team to pitch vertical marketing and convinced them that we could turn their business around, not just in color, but also in improving their black-and-white printing sales. And we did. The health-care market alone, which we managed, tripled Okidata's black-and-white printing sales in less than a year.

What's key here, and in all our pitches, was not just making bold claims. We also backed them up with information that provided solid answers to questions we knew a business either wasn't asking but should have been, or had asked but had not answered successfully. We never made empty promises when approaching potential clients, and that's why we landed—and kept—organizations like The Scotts Company, Carrier, and Benjamin Moore Paints. Intrigue got us a foot in the door, and when we walked through it, we had answers.

Intrigue

Intrigue, as a noun or a verb, involves mystery, curiosity, and fascination. When someone or something is intriguing, they are mysterious, curious, and fascinating. Intrigue can be superficial: the sort of glint on a shiny metal object that is, by itself, not terribly interesting. But intrigue can also be profound enough to be textured by nuance and layered with meaning. In those instances, intrigue is not a mere hook but a hint of something significant yet to come. Superficial intrigue is nothing more than sleight of hand used to mask a lack of depth. That's the sort of meaning people have in mind when they think of the negative definition of the word.[1]

In other words, intrigue created around something that is more interesting than the object, idea, or action itself merely leads to letdown. Unfortunately, that's what a lot of businesses do when they turn to marketing their service or product and focus more on the message—the intrigue—than on their brand and their purpose.

What's intriguing can also change over time. Consider for a moment anything that looks or behaves out of the ordinary. When I was a kid, no girls had nose piercings, let alone bolts through their eyebrows, belly buttons, nipples, or anywhere except their ears. Boys and young men had no piercings at all, certainly not diamond earring studs or tribal piercings. Today, though, these adornments are fairly commonplace. They barely raise an eyebrow, except perhaps in members of an older generation who can't help but wonder, "What, exactly, does that mean?"

What makes sustainable intrigue a powerful tool to help you connect with people in a meaningful way is that it has a payoff. When people ask me about why I have pink nail polish on my pinky, they may feel a variety of emotions about the story they hear. What they won't feel is somehow let down by the story behind the intrigue—the pink polish. That's because the two are linked in a meaningful way that anyone can understand. I'm sure there have been hundreds of people who have walked away from a conversation with me and done a bit of research. Of those, a considerable number have become actively involved in the Safe and Sound with Amaya project. I can't say how many have connected with the organization's purpose, but they have found their own ways to be involved in expressing their shared values. The point is that you can create intrigue that reflects what you are about and what you're trying to accomplish, and you hope it will resonate with others.

These days lots of stuff gets your attention, but it doesn't make you care. As a result, it's not sustainable. Part of sustainable success involves sustainable intrigue. As we've noted, making a visceral, emotional, personal connection is how you get and keep people involved. Heck, even the word, *visceral* hits you like a punch in the gut!

I know there are people out there who don't really care about children's safety. For whatever reason, they can't relate, so they're not going to be the people I pursue to get on board with my project. And you know what? That's okay. As I've mentioned once before in this book, it's the rest of you—the ones who are wiping tears from your faces when I tell you my story—I want.

But it's the broader issue—the impact of well-researched sustainable intrigue that makes a real connection—that I want you to keep in mind as you promote your own purpose.

Creating Connections Through Values

The Salvation Army is woven into the contemporary American holiday framework. We expect to see someone standing outside shops next to a red donation kettle, ringing a bell. But that scene wasn't always part of our thinking about the holidays. Begun in London in the mid-1800s, the Salvation Army had made its way as far west as San Francisco by the 1890s. Worried over people going hungry, Salvation Army Captain Joseph McFee hit upon the idea of donations, which he remembered had been successful in Liverpool, England, when he was a young sailor. McFee set out a pot with a placard next to it that read, "Keep the Pot Boiling."[2] Salvation Army Christmas dinners were the result, and within a decade a new tradition had been born. It was intriguing enough to take hold and still work more than 100 years later!

Today, people are finding new ways to give at the holidays. A 2013

West Jet Christmas video drew enormous attention to the Canadian airline, and for all the right reasons.[3] Passengers on two flights to Calgary had the opportunity to tell Santa what they wanted for Christmas by way of a live video feed that went straight to some West Jet "elves" waiting at the destination. While the flights were en route, these elves wrapped up toy cars for those who asked for a new, real one, and Ken dolls for those who said they were looking for husbands. Some gifts were even more extravagant. In all, 357 gifts came down the baggage ramp to unsuspecting travelers. The response was instantaneous and touching, and, best of all, it was authentic. Genuine connections were made between the givers and receivers.

When you listen to others and they listen to you, a connection is established. Creating intrigue, then, is a tool for connecting with people. The substance of your message doesn't change because you've enlisted an intriguing hook. People still think about the substance. But they often won't begin thinking about it until they can relate to it. Your values become meaningful to others once that connection is made.

Recall the example I mentioned in chapter 12 about the blind man whose fortunes changed with the rewording of his message. This simple yet powerful technique is not a gimmick; gimmicks don't last. Instead, it's a beginning. When FedEx made its promise to ship anything, anywhere around the world, within twenty-four hours, people scoffed. They don't scoff today. That's because the company didn't just issue an intriguing slogan. They made and delivered on an intriguing promise.

HOW I CREATE CONNECTIONS THROUGH MY VALUES

Like most everyone else, I value life. More specifically, I value protecting and preserving the lives of toddlers and young children, who tragically are gravely injured or killed daily by preventable accidents. That's because they're old enough to scamper around as they investigate their world but too young to understand the dangers around them.

Having suffered my own granddaughter's death in this way made me value life all over again. I gained a new purpose that sprang from my values: promoting home safety to protect and preserve the lives of toddlers and young children. I can't tell you whether or not I would have come to realize the same goal had our lives not been irrevocably altered. There are so many shocking and appalling events occurring daily in the world, just as there are so many beautiful and positively inspirational events, that it's hard to say what might have moved me to do something I would not otherwise have done.

People get involved in business for different reasons. Whether you're a hedge fund manager for billionaires or a micro-lender for poverty-stricken women in India, you are motivated to do what you do because there is something about the work that matters to you. I have built a career on helping people realize a vision for their business. First in marketing and advertising, and then in corporate speaking, I have made my success on a commitment to clearly articulated values and an unwavering purpose. If my values and purpose do not line up with a potential client's, we go no further together.

Having never previously experienced the death of a child or grand-child, I was impacted by the utter shock of Amaya's death, along with its circumstances, in a way I never could have realized otherwise. But the idea of using my polished fingernail to promote this serious cause didn't occur in a vacuum. It emerged out of my existing values, includ-ing an empathy for my fellow humans that pressed me into action and allowed me to do the most good.

Your Values Are Intriguing

When you're passionate about your ideas, you will almost invariably create interest, because I believe that values are always intriguing. People talk about and disagree over values endlessly. And people get into passionate discussions and disagreements about those values because these things are an essential feature of who we think we are as individuals, family members, community members, and citizens. Sometimes, people can be put off by that passion, especially if it's evangelical in nature. People generally don't want to be sold, pressured, or, worse still, made to feel like they're not doing the right thing if their vision doesn't match yours. I'm not talking about that kind of proselytizing passion. As I say, whenever someone asks me about my nail polish, "I don't want to push my agenda on you." All I do is tell my story. If people are interested enough to look up the Web site set up in support of the organization we created, or learn more about how to get involved in home safety issues, they can. What I've accomplished is to create intrigue.

Success Stories

We've already discussed a number of organizations that have created and sustained success through clearly articulated values and purposes. Let's look at some additional examples, this time with a focus on how each company used intrigue to support their work.

A big recent trend in the business world, especially in large corporations, is the decline of the hierarchical structure. Younger employees are more motivated to collaborate rather than to take direction from authority. Or if they do take direction, it's for the purpose of integrating an idea into the collaborative process. Part of this trend—it may be a cause or it may be a result—is changing technology in general and the rise of social media in particular.

Consider the increasing popularity of crowd sourcing to raise money for businesses, rather than seeking the traditional business loan from a bank. A Seattle, Washington, teenager named Jack Kim took that concept a step further by creating Benelab, a donation-generating search engine. The purpose of his venture, in which no adults are allowed, is "to make philanthropy easy and more accessible" by connecting it to an activity—Internet searches—that we engage in every day.[4] The intrigue lies within the simple and surprising way in which one can help others and be helped. What was once a complicated and difficult process is now done with a few keystrokes in a Google search.

Along with the emergence of social networking and the rise of organizations that create opportunities for philanthropic action and business profit, a tenuous economy has been equally important. Although the Great Recession was devastating to millions of people, some good has emerged from it. Among those who were laid off were a number of folks who had no idea how creative and entrepreneurial they could be until they decided to start a business.[5]

The question is obvious: Why begin such a risky venture when things are so rotten? Well, for one thing, according to Entrepreneur.com, not only are post-recession growth cycles longer than the recession itself, but there are other conditions that make starting up during hard times attractive. These include increases in qualified people ready to work, tax incentives that accrue to business owners, and the fact that everything tends to be cheaper during a recession, and so start-up costs are lower.[6] So, although the statistics on success don't favor companies founded during or immediately after a recession, there are advantages to taking the leap when times are especially rough.[7]

The United States has weathered multiple recessions—like the banking crises of the 1890s, the panic of 1907, and several downturns in the last fifty years—and, of course, the Great Depression. Some companies that we think of as woven into the fabric of the American story have begun in or after troubled times. Thomas Edison launched Edison General Electric in 1890.[8] IBM started out in 1896 as the Tabulating Machine Company.[9] In the twentieth century, there was General Motors (1908), Walt Disney Productions (1929), Revlon Cosmetics (1932), Tollhouse Cookies, (1933), Burger King (1953), Hyatt Hotels (1957), Federal Express (1971/1973), Microsoft (1975), and CNN (1980). Among the companies established during the most recent recession is Groupon (2008), which has become enormously successful.

If you live in a big city, no doubt you are familiar with the food truck, sometimes fondly referred to as "the roach coach." Until very recently, these kitchens on wheels were associated with construction sites and other places where it was just easier (or maybe necessary) for the food to come to you rather than for you to head to a restaurant. Well, in places like Los Angeles, the food truck industry has taken off. There are now gourmet mobile kitchens offering fare ranging from Vietnamese phó to Argentinian barbecue. According to a Kiplinger story,[10] the mobile business idea has quickly spread to other enterprises. Now there are mobile DNA and drug-testing labs, boxing clubs, hair salons, flower trucks, farm stands, tanning booths, and more! Here the intrigue is partly in the novelty, in using existing business models in new ways. But it's also in the experience itself. If you try a mobile hair salon and find the experience is really satisfying, you're more likely to use it again. Perhaps more importantly, the way you organize your day or think about how you navigate your world also changes in subtle but important ways. It's a kind of accidental social engineering, but it works!

The success of the mobile food industry is much like the success of Apple. These companies did not invent anything new; trucks and food existed for a long time. What they did, however, was to innovate the way trucks and food enhanced our lives. They took something we all knew, created intrigue around it, and followed it up with something that was greater than the initial intrigue. Steve Jobs and Apple did not invent the computer, the tablet, the cell phone, or retail shopping. What they did do was to innovate how all of those things made our lives better. When they created the initial advertising campaigns, which were definitely laced with intrigue and mystery, they followed it up with a user experience that paid off.

Sometimes intrigue is created accidentally, but wise leaders recognize it and run with it. That's arguably how the Hush Puppies brand re-emerged. As Malcolm Gladwell writes in The Tipping Point, by the early 1990s, the iconic shoe's sales were down to about 30,000 a year.[11] There was even talk of phasing out the footwear. Then everything changed.

New York City's always-hot club scene was the trend maker here. When word got out that the cool kids there were wearing Hush Puppies, other kids wanted to wear them as well. As word spread, fashion designers soon began putting the shoe in their runway shows from New York to Los Angeles. It was word of mouth that brought the Hush Puppies back. But let's not forget that, if the shoe weren't any good, it would never have lasted as long as it did in the first place, and its popularity would never have reignited. The club kids who brought the shoe back didn't have any agenda beyond wearing what was out of style. They certainly weren't trying to save the brand. But that's exactly what they did!

As we turn toward the final chapter of this book, consider the following question: When was the last time a business or individual did something to make you curious enough to want to know more?

CHAPTER 14

YOUR VALUES AND PURPOSE CAN COVER THE WORLD

ALWAYS ACT IN SUCH A WAY THAT YOU TREAT HUMANITY

ALWAYS AS AN END, AND NEVER MERELY AS A MEANS.

—IMMANUEL KANT

Not too long ago, I traveled on business to Amelia Island, Florida. An elderly gentleman named Carl picked me up at a resort there and drove me to the Jacksonville airport for my flight to Charleston, South Carolina, for the next leg of my trip.

What Carl Can Teach Us

The week had been an especially difficult time for me and my family, as it was the one-year anniversary of Amaya's death. As I made my way toward the car, Carl offered me a handshake and an enormous smile. "My name's Carl. How are you, my friend?"

His grin lit up the parking area and in an instant made me feel wonderful. We loaded my bags into the car and off we went. We started with small talk, but it wasn't long before he and I had learned much about each other.

Carl was a man of many talents and interests. He was the proprietor of the transportation company my client hired to bring me to the airport. He also owned a seafood company that ran two large shrimp boats. Then there was the cemetery headstone company.

Needless to say, Carl was full of energy. But he was also extraordinarily polite and gracious. As our conversation turned to personal matters, I thought about my wife and our daughter and wondered how they were holding up. Then Carl began to tell me the story of his life and losses.

His father was the pilot of the first American plane shot down at Pearl Harbor on December 7, 1941. Carl was only seven years old at the time. One of Carl's children had died in a car accident, just days after her high school graduation. Then there was the recent death of his seventeen-year-old grandson, shot in the woods while on a hunting trip.

I would have thought he'd become downcast thinking about all that pain. Instead, he said something I never expected: "Ya know, Mr. Deming, I'm a blessed man." He looked at me in the rear-view mirror, smiling at my surprised expression. "We've suffered some losses," he continued, "but so does everyone. Even with the losses, I have so much to be thankful for."

In that moment, Carl had reminded me that my family is among the billions around the world who suffer great losses and go through seemingly unbearable heartache every day. Our conversation made me reflect on Amaya and renewed the waves of grief that had hit me the moment I learned my granddaughter had died. But Carl also helped me to do something I hadn't done in a while. He helped me reconsider how I was dealing with the loss. Although my wife and I started a foundation to educate parents, grandparents, and caretakers of the risks in and around the home, I suddenly realized my attitude wasn't very healthy.

When I got home, I told my wife and daughter about Carl. They were as inspired as I was by his story and more importantly, by his outlook. Everyone has a story. Everyone goes through stuff. Everyone suffers heartache. And we basically have two choices when things go terribly wrong. We can either sink into self-pity, or we can forge ahead and try to inspire others to do the same. Carl is the sort of person who moves forward without forgetting those he loved, and he has inspired me to do the same. I want to be that smile and that handshake for everyone, because I'll never know if the hand I'm shaking has a story behind it. If so, I want them to walk away from our encounter feeling the way I did on the airport curb when Carl shook my hand, grabbed my shoulder, and said, "It has been such a pleasure and honor spending time with you. I hope you continue to have a blessed life."

What Makes an Idea Go Viral?

When I first started wearing my pink nail polish and talking about Amaya, it didn't take long before the information was global. Less than three days, in fact. From a *Huffington Post* article about my Pink Pinky to getting e-mails and Facebook posts and photos from people across the world who were painting their fingernails to show their support, my story went viral. It's a lot easier to accomplish this feat today than it was even as recently as twenty years ago. Before social media and the Internet, my encounter with Carl would have been, essentially, a one-person-at-a-time retelling of my story and would have reached very few individuals. Thanks to social media, e-mail blasts, and my personal blog, the story ended up reaching hundreds of thousands of people in an instant.

In this chapter, you'll learn how to marshal the power of traditional and social media to get the word out about your purpose, how to educate people, and how to keep the conversation going.

In the preceding chapters we've gone over the basics. We've already talked about intrigue, and specifically what I take that concept to mean. In other words, it's not about marketing, though that's a part of it. It's not about messaging, though that's a part of it. It's about authentic experience. And we've discussed the importance of connecting with each person individually and emotionally. There has to be solid information, too.

So it's simple. Make your message matter. Make your information meaningful, personal, and most important—emotional. As I've said over and over throughout this book, people cannot hear you, let alone absorb your information, until they feel you. A lot of wonderful, important, and potentially life-changing information has fallen on deaf ears, not because it wasn't great data, but because it wasn't communicated properly and effectively. So read on and learn how to use your emotional message in the many different outlets to reach the people you need to reach.

Harnessing the Power of Traditional and Social Media to Get the Word Out

The United States Postal Service traces its origins back to 1775, even before Independence. Benjamin Franklin was appointed the first Postmaster General, and his office was charged with ensuring "equal access to secure, efficient, and affordable mail service."[1] This was a pretty significant mission for his time, given not only the sheer size of the territory but also the challenges to safe and successful travel with important letters and other correspondence by foot, carriage, pony, or, later, rail. Amazingly, for centuries, our universal mail system has strengthened the bonds of friendship, family, and community through private letters expressing our most intimate feelings and legal documents that have changed the course of history. From the standpoint of today's astonishing technologies, which allow immediate and worldwide communication, the fact that people used to sit down and hand-write correspondence that then took weeks, if not months, to reach its destination seems unbelievable. But it's true.

When you look at the speed at which technology has developed in the past ten years—we now can communicate with robots on Mars!—the change is truly mind boggling. With each development in communications technologies comes insightful and innovative ways of developing our culture and expressing our values. The fact that we can reach more people, and reach them faster than ever before, provides us with new opportunities to share our values and purpose with others. But we have to be smart about how we do this. Remember, anyone with access to a computer and an Internet connection can conceivably communicate with billions of people. There's a lot of noise out there. Understanding how people use their communications devices—in particular how they use social media on those devices—will help guide us in the direction of harnessing their power.

It seems like people spend greater amounts of time interacting on social media sites than they do IRL ("in real life"). Facebook, YouTube, LinkedIn, Instagram, Twitter, Pinterest, deviantART, Flickr, Tumblr, Yelp, or any of the hundreds of other social media sites out there . . .

each has its own look, culture, and demographic. They all have their roots in message and chat boards, virtual places where people could congregate to exchange information.

So, what are companies doing to harness the power of this new technology and get the word out? According to a Harvard Business Review white paper, businesses are not taking full advantage of the communicative power of social media. "Despite the vast potential social media brings, many companies seem focused on social media activity primarily as a one-way promotional channel, and have yet to capitalize on the ability to not only listen to, but analyze, consumer conversations and turn the information into insights that impact the bottom line."[2]

I have long argued that a company's commitment to over-delivering on its promise to excellent customer service is what makes a brand successful. A commitment to excellent customer service is a value—or should be—for every organization. (We know the old saying about a dissatisfied customer telling ten people how awful his experience was; in the Internet age that saying has been modified to ten million.[3] Just ask businesses that have crossed the negative threshold on sites like Yelp and Angie's List.) Whatever motivates your commitment to this value, social networking sites are upping the ante.

According to a Mashable.com article,[4] the videos that went viral in the first part of 2013 each had a key element: People felt they could viscerally relate to some value in it. For example, we are more likely to share a video that "contains something deeply human," such as heartfelt interviews about how our perceptions of ourselves don't always match what others see. That was the focus of a Dove commercial that was shared by millions of people. An element of mystery also gets us talking, was the case with a Pepsi commercial in which a car salesman was taken on a test drive by disguised race car driver Jeff Gordon. What many wondered was whether or not the salesman was actually in on the prank. A simply produced YouTube video on wealth inequality in America[5] used charts and graphics in a way that demonstrated the shocking disparity between the richest and poorest people in the United States. These are only a few of the handful of videos that the article discussed, but their diversity shows that people connect with all sorts of topics, if the way those topics are presented really does get us in the gut.

That has been my point up until now, and it will be our focus in the coming pages: No matter what form of media you use, and no matter how much the technology changes, what makes your message effective remains constant—authenticity and emotion.

Before getting into the dos and don'ts of advertising and marketing, let me make a very strong recommendation: Hire a professional! Crafting an effective and efficient marketing strategy has always been a complicated process. Take it from me; I spent most of my life doing it. And today it's even more complicated than it used to be. With the growing and ever changing social media landscape in the mix, hiring a marketing expert or advertising agency to handle the marketing and media details gives you the space you need to do what you do best— manage and grow your organization. That said, even if you do hire a professional, it's always good to have a solid grasp of what's going on, how things work, and what your options are. So let's take an overview look at what you might encounter in this field.

Traditional Media

What was once cutting-edge technology is now considered "traditional media." Newspapers, magazines, direct mail, and television and radio are still viable and necessary, but careful consideration must be given to each to assure a cost-effective approach.

PRINT MEDIA

Magazine and newspaper readership continues to drop, as online readership and subscriptions continue to rise. Consequently, as production costs rise and advertisers vanish, newspapers and magazines across the country are closing shop. You can get good deals in print media these days, but take a very close and careful look at readership and distribution. First and foremost, be sure the paper or magazine you're considering reaches your target audience. A glossy, cool ad is meaningless if the people who notice it aren't potential customers. You may see or hear impressive "reach" numbers such as a 500,000 circulation or a 1,000,000 readership, but, again, be sure the majority of those people are within your target audience. Paying for high reach numbers could be very costly if you're reaching the wrong people.

DIRECT MAIL

Direct mail is a very cost-effective way to reach a specific target audience. With direct mail, you can research and identify your audience by location, age, gender, income, and so on, and purchase a highly targeted list. With this information at hand, it's easy to get your direct-mail piece into the hands of those most likely to buy your product or join your cause. However, I must caution you about the actual direct-mail product. Do not create something that you like. Create something your readers will like; more importantly, create something that they will respond to. Go back to my discussion in the previous chapter about creating intrigue for a more detailed discussion of what I mean.

You don't want to pay for the research, list, postage, and printing if the message isn't truly effective.

ELECTRONIC MEDIA/TELEVISION AND RADIO

The most important thing to keep in mind with electronic media is reach and frequency. But once again, be sure you're reaching the right people. You'll meet a lot of radio and television sales reps with numbers to prove they're the number-one station for your demographics. A word to the wise: I've never met the number-two station in my market! It's also true that television typically has very large coverage. That's good, right? Perhaps, but if you're a local company, drawing customers from a very specific and small geographic area, surely you don't want to be paying for a commercial that reaches seven counties. They'll sell you reach and frequency numbers, but you may very well be reaching more people than you need to. The same holds true for radio. Look at the listeners within your target audience; find out when they're listening and what they're listening to. A good way to judge whether or not you're making the right media selection is to survey your customers and even your employees. Track who's doing what, how often, and how consistently. Then work that information into your marketing and media strategy.

Social Media

Here we go! My friends, I'm going to be honest with you about something. As of this writing, I am fifty-six years of age. I'm fairly savvy with technology, but compared to my kids and the younger people working with me and for me, I'm a dinosaur! What I mean by this is the technology came at me—at all of us of a certain age—at an astonishing rate of speed, and it continues to change daily, offering new and improved options for reaching others online. As a result, I have difficulty discerning the good options from bad, the viable ones from those I should ignore. The difference between the younger generation and me is that I had to re-learn how I learn. I had to literally change my behavior and my comfort levels when it came to technology. My kids, on the other hand, and young adults everywhere, grew up with this technology.

Just as using a phone or changing the channel on the television is second nature to me, learning new technology and navigating through the complicated processes and landscapes of social media is second nature to them. I have an advertising agency now that manages my online programs. I have some control over the technology so that I can change content when I want, but they manage the platforms and my online presence. Here again, unless you're an expert at social media, either hire a person within your company to manage it or use an agency. Social media is too much of a moving target to keep up with if you're trying to run your business or nonprofit organization.

The basics are not that different, beginning with message and placement. After all, the principles of marketing haven't changed; it's the mechanisms for effective implementation of those principles that have.

Remember, what you do must be authentic, not superficially intriguing. Sure, it may be the case that you can script something that looks authentic and then goes viral, but only the real thing has the lasting impact. Often, that means there's a purpose that reconnects us with what truly matters. For example, knowing he did not have long to live, a seventeen-year-old boy dying of cancer wrote an incredibly sweet and catchy song for his parents. Zach Sobiech's "Cloud" is irrepressibly hopeful, both in its lyrical content and musical arrangement. The direct and honest way in which Sobiech shares himself is what made the video, and a subsequent song, "Fix Me Up," so successful. He died on May 20, 2013, but he continues to connect with and influence people through his music.

With that in mind, let's take a brief look at some social media precepts.

Since I don't feel I'm savvy enough in this realm to advise you in a meaningful way, I've asked my good friend Shawn Comer to help me out. Shawn is president and CEO of Mindshare Marketing Group in Syracuse, New York,[6] a full-service advertising and marketing agency, with a strong focus and expertise in the electronic and social media disciplines. Here are his thoughts on social media:

IT'S ALL ABOUT YOUR STORY

You need to find the people who will think your story matters and build a community around your cause. There's never been a time in history with more accessible tools to take your story to the world. Social media has become ubiquitous, and for grass-roots efforts, it's a great place to start. From Facebook to Twitter to LinkedIn, to name a few, a great amount of thought and innovation has gone into the development of these tools. All have been developed in the name of better connecting the world. You might as well leverage the labors of a lot of very bright folks.

MAKE YOUR STORY MATTER

You need to make your story clear and relevant while making it easy for people to engage and participate in it. You'll want to build a well-defined identity and be able to explain simply why others should be interested in your cause. It's worth investing the time and resources to thoroughly work through the development of your brand identity and your story before you launch your endeavor. If possible, be iconic. A pink pinky, a pink ribbon . . . those are memorable symbols that can grow to represent a specific cause. Done well, they can speak volumes. Remember, you'll likely be living with your identity, for better or worse, for years to come. When it comes to your story, be open, be real, be honest, and be emotional but never be over the top. With a little push, an engaging story with enough depth and empathy will start to tell itself over time as others engage with it and share their stories.

FIND THE PEOPLE WHO MATTER TO YOU

Have a Web site, even if it's just a modest one. Like Facebook, a Web site establishes some online real estate where people can find you and learn about your cause. In this day and age, it's a big credibility check for people to make sure that you and your cause are real and worth a look. The site can also become the focal point of your outreach efforts and a real-time resource for sharing news and events for your cause. It will allow you to encourage visitors to sign up for future updates. Self-generated e-mail lists can become a very valuable asset over the long haul. From a home base of a robust Facebook page, an active Twitter presence, and a functional Web site, there are literally a million things you can do to target and reach out to the people who may connect with your purpose.

BUILD YOUR COMMUNITY

People need a reason to engage. And once they do, they need even more reasons to get involved or support your goal. Facebook offers a great environment for this. It's engaging, it's personal, the information is real-time, and it's relatively easy to keep it fresh with new content. The quality of your content is the key to your success on Facebook.

Remember, you're having a running conversation with everyone who "likes" you. With the advent of tools like promoted posts on Facebook, it's becoming easier to quickly expand your audience.

Twitter is essentially a personal PR engine that can allow your messages, thoughts, and news to ripple through to your followers and beyond, thanks to the retweets of others. Again, how well you present your purpose, how active you are on Twitter, and how compelling your cause is, will all help drive your success in building and retaining your community. Like any other community, much of social media is driven by pockets of key influencers. Follow the folks who you want to have follow you on Twitter. "Like" the folks who you want to have like you on Facebook. You get the point. You have to be active and fully engaged in social media to maximize the benefits.

DON'T BE AFRAID TO ASK FOR HELP

At the beginning, it might not seem that you have the available resources to master social media, but a little help can go a long way, particularly in the digital space. You'll eliminate years of research, trial and error, and, potentially, wasted efforts. You need to spend your time building your brand, connecting with people, and telling your story, not becoming an expert in the finer points of social, digital, and traditional media tactics. Whether you find a smart freelance marketer who knows the digital landscape and can handle social media and small digital campaigns, or you hire a large, fully integrated agency, professional help makes sense in most circumstances. Either way, these are folks who think about this stuff all day, every day. Who knows? They may become a fan of your purpose as well and offer to participate at pro bono rates.

If you think about what Shawn is saying, you'll see the resemblances to the concepts I've been talking about all through this book: Know your values, articulate your purpose, find the people who resonate with it and create a culture around it, then connect emotionally and authentically with the world at large.

Pulling It All Together Again

Since long before my first book, *The Brand Who Cried Wolf*, was published, I have been on a mission. It's simple. I want people to start treating each other like people again. For me, that means treating others as inherently dignified, worthy of respect, worthy of honesty and fairness, and worthy of compassion. And you know what? When you treat people this way, nine times out of ten, they live up to your expectations.

I've already told you that I was twenty-six years old when I started my first company. What you don't know is how I understood my purpose when I undertook that project. From the beginning, my personal goal was to promote the idea that business, like other areas of our lives, must be devoted to the highest levels of respect for customers, clients, coworkers, employers, and employees. That's what makes me tick. When my company received a thank-you note from a client, I would gather the whole office around to read it to them. Why? Because making a positive difference in someone's life—positive enough that they took the time to express their appreciation for a job they were already paying my company to do—has always mattered more to me than anything else. "If I didn't have to make money to pay your salaries and make a living," I'd tell my staff, "I'd be happy just getting these letters."

As I wrote earlier in this book, I love business. I love what it stands for, or at least what it could and should stand for. I love that someone can have an idea and use all their passion and smarts and hard work and make a go of it. I've been involved in business at many levels throughout my professional career, and I've seen people and companies come and go. But those that are sustainable seem to always have one thing in common: service above profit. They were in it for something bigger than the financial bottom line or their name on a symphony program. They were in it because they had a purpose.

As a businessman for many years, I not only understand financial profit as a necessity, I believe in financial profit as a means to continually create a meaningful purpose in other areas of your personal and professional life. If you think about it, profit and purpose can be interchangeable—if, in fact, you think of them as interchangeable. In other words, consider profit as something much larger than simply the bottom line. Doing so will have you not only thinking in larger terms but also working and living that way as well.

The true bottom line is this: The best way to be a success in whatever you do is to live your purpose through your values every day. You cannot compartmentalize those values when you leave your home or family and head out into the world. If I have accomplished just one thing through this book, I hope it is helping you to realize you cannot separate who you are from what you do. The sooner you know what your purpose and values are and how you can live these through all your relationships, the more successful a person you will be.

I'm so pleased and honored that you took the time to read this book. I truly, truly hope that it has taught you, touched you, and helped you to better understand your values and achieve your purpose, whatever your purpose may be. I am humbled.

NOTES

Prologue

1. The Consumers Product Safety Commission issued a report in 2012 (http://www.cpsc.gov//PageFiles/135118/tipover2012.pdf) stating that, between 2000 and 2011, 349 children had been killed in accidents involving falling furniture. That averages to twenty-nine preventable deaths a year. In 2011 alone, the number was forty-one, or one every nine days. Of additional concern is the fact that these figures are *increasing* over time, not decreasing.

2. "Safe and Sound with Amaya" http://safeandsoundwithamaya.org/.

Chapter 2

1. Jacobellis v. Ohio, 378 US 184 (1964), http://www.law.cornell.edu /supremecourt/text/378/184

2. Michael E. Porter and Mark R. Kramer, "Creating Shared Values," *Harvard Business Review Online*, January 2011, http://hbr.org/2011/01/the-big-idea -creating-shared-value.

3. Steve Strauss, "Business values are good for profits . . . and you, too," *USA Today*, May 22, 2011, http://usatoday30.usatoday.com/money/smallbusiness /columnist/strauss/2011-05-22-strauss-business-values_n.htm.

Chapter 3

1. Those who make this latter claim might say, for example, that since it's impossible to help everyone in a similar situation, it seems arbitrary to help one person and not another. We will discuss this sort of reasoning in chapter 8, when we focus on values and critical thinking.

2. Diana Rowland, "Your Japanese Business Card," Linguist.com, www.linguist.com/services-japanese-card.htm.

3. This example is not out of the ordinary—it's a version of similar stories from a non-US country.

Chapter 4

1. Brian Dakss, "Autistic Teen's Hoop Dreams Come True," CBSnews. com, February 23, 2006, http://www.cbsnews.com/news/autistic-teens-hoop-dreams-come-true/.

Chapter 5

1. "Why Pioneer," Pioneerbasement.com http://www.pioneerbasement.com/ethics.php

2. Quoted in Melisa Morton, "Good Ethics Pay Off" in *Permanent Buildings & Foundations Magazine* (January 2006).

Chapter 6

1. "Enhanced F Scale for Tornado Damage," Spc.com, http://www.spc.noaa.gov/faq/tornado/ef-scale.html

2. John Flesher and Alan S. Zagier, "Joplin Tornado Leaves Environmental Hazards in Aftermath," *Huffpost Green*, May 31, 2011, http://www.huffingtonpost.com/2011/05/31/joplin-tornado-environmental-hazards_n_868991.html.

3. "Taking Care: Corporate Responsibility," Ironmountain.com, http://www. ironmountain.com/Company/Corporate-Responsibility.aspx

4. Cy Wakeman, "Your Ego and the Bad Decissions it Makes," *Forbes Online*, March 4, 2013, http://www.forbes.com/sites/cywakeman/2013/03/04/your -ego-and-the-bad-decisions-it-makes/.

5. See also August Tukar, "CEOs, Egos and Logos: Overcoming the Sudden Squalls of Leadership," *Forbes Online*, April 11, 2011, http://www.forbes. com/sites/augustturak/2011/04/11/ceos-egos-and-logos-overcoming- the-sudden-squalls-of-leadership/, in which August Turak makes a nice comparison between monasteries' business success and the monastic practice of detachment.

6. "Real California Milk," http://www.realcaliforniamilk.com/.

7. Max H. Bazerman, George Loewenstein, and Don A. Moore, "Why Good Accountants Do Bad Audits," *Harvard Business Review* 80.11 (November 2002), pp. 96–102.

Chapter 7

1. Mike Myatt, "10 Reasons Your Top Talent Will Leave You," *Forbes Online*, December 13, 2012, http://www.forbes.com/sites/mikemyatt/2012/12/13/10 -reasons-your-top-talent-will-leave-you/. Emphasis added.

2. Doris Kearns Goodwin, *Team of Rivals: The Political Genius of Abraham Lincoln* (New York: Simon & Schuster, 2005).

3. Doris Kearns Goodwin, "Defeat Your Opponents. Then Hire Them," *The New York Times Online*, August 3, 2008, http://www.nytimes.com/2008/08/03 /opinion/03goodwin.html?pagewanted=print&_r=0.

4. Michael Burlingame, "The Patriot-Statesman," *The Wall Street Journal Online*, September 14, 2012, http://online.wsj.com/article/SB1000087239639044381 9404577635400729428124.html.

5. Ram Charan, Jerry Useem, and Ann Harrington, " Why Companies Fail CEOs," CNN.com, May 27, 2002, http://money.cnn.com/magazines/fortune /fortune_archive/2002/05/27/323712/.

6. Daniel Goleman, Richard Boyatzis, and Annie McKee, *Primal Leadership: Learning to Lead with Emotional Intelligence* (Boston: Harvard Business Review Press, 2004).

7. Justin Fox, "Why the Government Wouldn't Let AIG Fail," Time Online, September 16, 2008, http://www.time.com/time/business/ article/0,8599,1841699,00.html.

8. See, for example, Serena NG and Joann S. Lublin, "AIG Chief Is Being Treated for Cancer," *Wall Street Journal Online*, October 26, 2010, http://online.wsj. com/news/articles/SB10001424052702303467004575574703836744636.

Chapter 8

1. http://www.davey.com/about/pr/news/do-it-right-or-not-at-all.aspx

2. "SAS Institute CEO Jim Goodnight on Building Strong Companies—and a More Competitive U.S. Workforce," University of Pennsylvania, January 5, 2011, http://knowledge.wharton.upenn.edu/article.cfm?articleid=2660

3. Charles Fishman, "Sanity Inc.," *Fast Company Online*, December 31, 1998, http://www.fastcompany.com/36173/sanity-inc

4. Scott Deming.com, http://www.scottdeming.com/

Chapter 9

1. See, for example, Raymond Fisman, "CEO Right: Yahoo workers Must Show Up," CNN.com, March 2, 2013, http://www.cnn.com/2013/02/26/opinion /fisman-yahoo.

2. "Why I am Quitting Facebook," originally published on CNN. com on February 25, 2013. See also http://www.forbes.com/sites/ anthonykosner/2013/01/21/facebook-is-recycling-your-likes-to-promote -stories-youve-never-seen-to-all-your-friends/.

3. "Beware of Dissatisfied Consumers: They Like to Blab," University of Pennsylvania, March 8, 2006, http://knowledge.wharton.upenn.edu/article. cfm?articleid=1422.

4. George H. Labovitz and Victor Rosansky, "The Big Picture: The Alignment Framework," *Training Magazine Online*, February 6, 2013, http://www. trainingmag.com/content/big-picture-alignment-framework.

5. See, for example, Everett Rogers, *Diffusion of Innovations* (New York: Free Press, 1962); Daryl Conner, *Managing at the Speed of Change: How Resilient Managers Succeed and Prosper where Others Fail* (New York: Random House, 1993); and Linda Ackerman Anderson and Dean Anderson, *Beyond Change Management: Advanced Strategies for Today's Transformational Leaders* (New York: John Wiley & Sons, 2002).

Chapter 10

1. "Who is This Steve Guy Everybody's Always Talking About?" Chipotle Corporation, http://www.chipotle.com/en-us/chipotle_story/steves_story /steves_story.aspx. All quotations from Ells are from this page.

2. See, for example, "Industrial Livestock Production," Grace Communications Foundation, http://www.sustainabletable.org/859/industrial-livestock- production.

3. Danielle Sacks, "Most Innovative Companies 2012: 34_Chipotle," *Fast Company Magazine Online*, February 7, 2012, http://www.fastcompany.com /most-innovative-companies/2012/chipotle

4. Motley Fool Staff, "Live Chat: Chipotle Co-CEO Monty Moran," Fool.com, December 14, 2010, http://www.fool.com/investing/high-growth/2010/12/14 /live-chat-chipotle-co-ceo-monty-moran.aspx.

5. Gary Strauss, "Chipotle Co-CEOs Gorge on Fat 2012 Paydays, Stock Gains," *USA Today Online*, March 17, 2013, http://www.usatoday.com/story/money/business/2013/03/15/chipotle-co-ceos-get-massive-2012-paydays/1991671/.

6. Adapted from Joshua D. Margolis, "The Responsibility Gap," in *The Hedgehog Review: Critical Reflections on Contemporary Culture*, Summer 2009 (Vol. 11, No. 2): 41–53.

7. Alexis Lai, "World's Most Corrupt Place to Do Business is . . .," *Business 360* (blog), CNN.com, November 3, 2011, http://business.blogs.cnn.com/2011/11/03/world-most-corrupt-place-to-do-business-is/.

8. "World Report 2013: China," Human Rights Watch, http://www.hrw.org/world-report/2013/country-chapters/china.

9. "History," Wal-Mart Corporation, http://corporate.walmart.com/our-story/heritage

10. "Sam Walton," Wal-Mart Corporation, http://corporate.walmart.com/our-story/heritage/sam-walton.

11. See, for example, Charles Fishman, "The Wal-Mart You Don't Know," *Fast Company Online*, December 1, 2003, http://www.fastcompany.com/47593/wal-mart-you-dont-know.

12. "Making Change at Walmart," www.walmartwatch.com.

13. "Wal-Mart in Crisis: How the World's Largest Retailer Lost Its Way," *A Wal-Mart Watch Report* (blog), p. 2, June 2007, http://walmartwatch.com/wp-content/blogs.dir/2/files/pdf/growth_report.pdf.

14. Sue Shellenbarger, "How Could a Sweet Third-Grader Just Cheat on That School Exam?" *The Wall Street Journal Online*, May 15, 2013, http://online.wsj.com/article/SB10001424127887324216004578483002751090818.html.

15. Joshua Margolis, "The Responsibility Gap, " in *The Hedgehog Review: Critical Reflections on comtemporary Culture*, Summer 2009 (Vol. 11, No. 2): 45.

16. Ibid., 43. Margolis identifies three versions of the gap, each of which is relevant to a number of points I make in this book: 1) "the discrepancy between the documented limitations in human beings' functioning and the complex set of responsibilities those in business must meet" (p. 45); 2) "There is a discrepancy between the responsibilities business school graduates encounter at each stage of their careers and what they are equipped to handle...the next demand or level of responsibility often outstrips what individuals are ready to take on" (p. 45); 3) There is a discrepancy between the reality of human conduct and ethical ideals (p. 50).

17. Ibid., 41, 43.

18. Ibid., 45.

19. See, for example, Antonio R. D'Amasio, *Descartes' Error: Emotion, Reason and the Human Brain* (New York: Penguin Books, 2005).

20. Margolis ("Leadership Gap") offers a solid selection of the literature in 2009. See his footnotes on pp. 48–49.

21. Ibid., 47. "Ideally we want to access our intuitive, emotional responses without short-circuiting our deliberative capacity or trampling our deliberative conclusions. We also want to be able to activate our deliberative capacity without thereby discarding our emotional responses."

22. Ibid., 48–49.

23. Ibid., 48. Margolis cites a study by Daylian M. Cain, George Lowenstein, and Don A. Moore, "The Dirt on Coming Clean: Perverse Effects of Disclosing Conflicts of Interest," in the *Journal of Legal Studies* 34.1 (2005), pp. 1–25.

24. U.S. Display Group, http://www.usdisplaygroup.com/.

25. "About," U.S. Display Group, http://www.usdisplaygroup.com/about/: "We will strive to be our Customers' vendor of choice by providing a superior quality product at a fair price, and by demonstrating innovation, exceptional customer service, and a value added approach to our Customers in everything we do."

26. Toms Corporation, http://www.toms.com/our-movement/

Chapter 11

1. John Tierney, "Do You Suffer From Decision Fatigue?" *The New York Times Magazine Online*, August 17, 2011, http://www.nytimes.com/2011/08/21/magazine/do-you-suffer-from-decision-fatigue.html?pagewanted=all

2. Ibid.

3. Ibid.

4. Vohs, et al, "Decision Fatigue Exhausts Self-Regulatory Resources," *Psychology Today Online*, p.3 www.psychologytoday.com/files/.../584/decision200602-15vohs.pdf.

5. Barry Schwartz, *The Paradox of Choice: Why More is Less* (New York: Harper Perennial, 2005).

6. John Tierney, "Do You Suffer From Decision Fatigue?' *The New York Times Magazine Online*, August 17, 2011, http://www.nytimes.com/2011/08/21/magazine/do-you-suffer-from-decision-fatigue.html?pagewanted=all. This scenario reminds me of a story an acquaintance told me. While in graduate school in the late 1990s, my acquaintance hosted two new students who had just arrived to start their PhD program. One was from Belgrade, Serbia, and the other was from Vilnius, Lithuania. Neither student had ever been to the United States, and both came from parts of the world where choices were severely limited. She took them to the grocery store, pointed them in the direction they wanted to go (bread), and told them she'd meet up with them at the checkout line. When they didn't show up after twenty minutes, she went to search for them, only to find them standing in front of shelf after shelf of bread. They looked at her in utter disbelief and no small amount of consternation. "What do we do?" they asked. Eventually, she chose bread she thought they'd like, and they continued to buy the same brand for as long as she knew them.

7. "What Do You Value?" The Values Institute, http://www.thevaluesinstitute.org/. This is a self-described think tank run out of the Southern California advertising and marketing firm, DGWB.

8. Paula Andruss, "Secrets of the 10 Most-Trusted Brands," *Entrepreneur Magazine Online*, March 20, 2012, http://www.entrepreneur.com/article/223125.

9. Ibid.

10. Scott Deming, *The Brand Who Cried Wolf: Deliver on Your Company's Promise and Create Customers for Life* (New York: Wiley, 2010).

11. Howard Schulz and Dori Jones Yang, *Pour Your Heart Into It: How Starbucks Built a Company One Cup at a Time* (New York: Hyperion Books, 1999)

12. Paula Andruss, "Secrets of the 10 Most-Trusted Brands," *Entrepreneur Magazine Online*, March 20, 2012, http://www.entrepreneur.com/article/223125.

13. "Chimps & Bonobos," The Hominid Psychology Research Group at the Max Planck Institute for Evolutionary Biology, http://www.eva.mpg.de/3chimps/files/apes.htm.

14. Frans de Waal, *The Bonobo and the Atheist* (New York: W. W. Norton & Co., 2013). See also Frans de Waal, *Primates and Philosophers: How Morality Evolved* (Princeton: Princeton University Press, 2009) and *Good Natured: The Origins of Right and Wrong in Humans and Other Animals* (Boston: Harvard University Press, 1997).

15. "Chimpanzees Not as Selfish as We Thought," Discovery News, August 8, 2011, http://news.discovery.com/animals/chimps-share-110808.htm.

16. If you think the evolutionary account of morality is wanting and believe instead that a religious account is accurate, you can still agree that there are these baseline values that share the same source—whatever that source is.

17. Ashoka, "Empathy in Busineness: Indulgence or Invaluable?" *Forbes Online*, March 22, 2013, http://www.forbes.com/sites/ashoka/2013/03/22/empathy-in-business-indulgence-or-invaluable/.

18. "Company Info: Our History," Patagonia Inc., http://www.patagonia.com/us/patagonia.go?assetid=3351

19. Ibid.

20. Quoted in Mark Lefko, *Unlock the Power of Your Team* (Atlanta: Lefko Group, 2009), p. 15. Available at http://www.unlockthepower.net/

21. "Becoming a Responsible Company," Patagonia Inc., http://www.patagonia.com/us/patagonia.go?assetid=2329

22. Tamara Schweitzer, " How to Build a Values-Driven Business," Inc.com, http://www.inc.com/guides/2010/03/social-enterprise.html

Chapter 12

1. See, for example, "Giving Back to Those Who Have Given So Much," www.leavenoveteranbehind.org.

2. See, for example, Lisa Earle McCloud's concise article, "How to Get People to Buy Into Your Ideas," *Huffpost Business*, December 13, 2011, http://www.huffingtonpost.com/lisa-earle-mcleod/how-to-get-people-to-buy-_b_1145696.html

3. Jeb Blount, *People Buy You: The Real Secret to what Matters Most in Business* (New York: John Wiley & Sons, 2010).

4. Ibid., 2.

5. Peter Barron Stark and Jane Flaherty, *Engaged! How Leaders Build Organizations Where Employees Love to Come to Work* (San Diego: Bentley Press, 2009).

6. CV Harquail, "Acknowledge, Affirm, and Amplify Good Business Practices," Authentic Organizations, May22, 2014, http://authenticorganizations.com/.

7. "Blind Man: The Power of Words We Use," http://www.youtube.com/watch?v=YfNO3rd1Pcg

8. Michael E. Porter and Mark R. Kramer, "Creating Shared Value," *Harvard Business Review Online*, January 2011, http://hbr.org/2011/01/the-big-idea-creating-shared-value.

9. "The concept of shared value can be defined as policies and operating practices that enhance the competitiveness of a company while simultaneously advancing the economic and social conditions in the communities in which it operates. Shared value creation focuses on identifying and expanding the connections between societal and economic progress. The concept rests on the premise that both economic and social progress must be addressed using value principles. Value is defined as benefits relative to costs, not just benefits alone. Value creation is an idea that has long been recognized in business, where profit is revenues earned from customers minus the costs incurred. However, businesses have rarely approached societal issues from a value perspective but have treated them as peripheral matters. This has obscured the connections between economic and social concerns."

Chapter 13

1. For example, Webster's dictionary offers one negative definition each for the word as a noun and a verb: "a secret scheme," and "the practice of engaging in secret schemes."

2. "Red Kettle History," The Salvation Army USA, http://salvationarmyusa.org/usn/red-kettle-history

3. Kim Peterson, "WestJet's Holiday Video Becomes an Online Sensation," CBSNews.com, December 16, 2013, http://www.cbsnews.com/news/westjets-holiday-video-becomes-an-online-sensation/.

4. "Bene." Search engine, http://benelab.org/.

5. Spencer E. Ante, "Fertile Ground for Startups," *Bloomberg Businessweek Magazine*, November 12, 2009, http://www.businessweek.com/magazine/content/09_47/b4156046735817.htm.

6. Brad Sugars, "Top 10 Reasons to Start a Business in a Recession," *Entrepreneur Magazine Online*, February 24, 2009, http://www.entrepreneur.com/article/200342.

7. Kimberly Weisul, "We're in a Recession. Time to Start a Company," Inc.com, November 17, 2011 http://www.inc.com/www.inc.com/articles/201111/were-in-a-recession-time-to-start-a-company.html.

8. "Thomas Edison @ GE," General Electric, http://www.ge.com/about-us/history/thomas-edison

9. "Chronological History of IBM," IBM.com, http://www03.ibm.com/ibm/history/history/decade_1890.html.

10. "8 Intriguing Businesses on Wheels," *Kiplinger Magazine* Online, http://www.kiplinger.com/slideshow/business/T049-S001-8-intriguing-businesses-on-wheels/index.html.

11. Malcolm Gladwell, *The Tipping Point: How Little Things Can Make a Big Difference* (New York: Back Bay Books, 2002), pp. 3–7.

Chapter 14

1. Publication 100, The United States Postal Service—an American History 1775-2006, http://about.usps.com/publications/pub100/pub100_001.htm.

2. Harvard Business Review Analytics Services, "The New Conversation: Taking Social Media from Talk to Action," (Harvard Business School Publishing, 2010), Executive Summary. See also Megan Ennis, "Social Media: What Most Companies Don't Know," *Harvard Business Review Online,* http://hbr.org/web/slideshows/social-media-what-most-companies-dont-know/1-slide.

3. Paul Gillin, *The New Influencers: A Marketer's Guide to the New Social Media* (Fresno: Linden Publishing, 2007).

4. Seth Fiegerman, "Here's Why These 6 Videos Went Viral," Mashable.com, May 15, 2013, http://mashable.com/2013/05/15/viral-video-factors/.

5. "Wealth Inequality in America," video, https://www.youtube.com/watch?v=QPKKQnijnsM.

6. "Work Smart," Mindshare.com, www.mindsharellc.com.

INDEX

A

Accidents, killing of toddlers by preventable, 3–4
Accountability, promoting, 110–113
Activities, values-driven, 152–160
Adams, Abigail, 21
Advanced Distributor Products, 73, 102–104
AIG, 87–89
Alignment, 115–116
Altruism, empathy-based, 146
Amaya, death of, 2–7, 159–160, 167, 173, 179
Amazon.com, 112, 140, 141
Andras, Stephen, 57–58
Angelou, Maya, 137
Angie's List, 184
Apple Inc., 133, 140, 142, 177
Arnold, Matthew, 91
Assumptions
    asking for help in uncovering unstated, 62
    in creating dialogue, 116
    dangers of making, 61–62
Attitude
    can-do, 143
    just do it, 143
Attorney-client privilege, 37–38
Authenticity, 156
    craving for, 140

B

Background checks, 77
Banking business, staying out of, 95
Banking crises, 176
Bates, Edward, 82–83
Beliefs, psychological power of, 49
Beneficence, 34
Benelab, 175
Benjamin Moore Paints, 169
Benmosche, Robert, 88–89

Blind transfer, 51
Boston Marathon bombings, 130
Bottom-up approach to culture, 28
Branding, 142
    emotional connections in, 147
The Brand Who Cried Wolf (Deming), 9–10, 49, 192
Breaking even, 11
Burger King, 176
Business
    being popular in dealings with, 96
    financial profit as goal of, 11
    growing, 57–58
    making decisions that impact, 67
    reasons for getting involved in, 13
    starting a new, 15–16
    values in, 15, 27–29, 89–90, 132
    connection between individual values and, 27–28

C

Can-do attitude, 143
Capitalism, 10–11
    redefining, 15
Career goals, alignment with employers, 80
Carrier, 169
Case studies
    aligning values and purpose in, 123–124
    Chipotle Mexican Grill, 122–123
    critical thinking during a crisis, 68–69
    culture of creativity: SAS, 98–99
    culture of routine: U.S. Display Group, 99–102
    Davey Tree Expert Company, 92–98
    in defining values: my ad agency, 29–31
    derailed purposes in, 124–126
    "Flower Power" Flower Shop, 18–19
    justifying values, 36–42
    Patagonia, 148–149
    shared-values: my ad agency, 81–82

Walmart, 126–128
yes man: the AIG meltdown and a
    turnaround, 87–89
Change
    attempting incremental, 119
    management of, 117–119
    resistance to, 118
Chase, Salmon P., 82
Chipotle Mexican Grill, 121, 122–123, 162
    values, purposes and action grid for, 135
Chomsky, Noam, 67
Chouinard, Yvon, 148–149
Chouinard Equipment, 148
Clients
    investigating complaints made by, 93–94
    thinking of first, 93
"Cloud," 188
CNN, 176
Coca-cola, 140, 141–142
    rollout of New Coke, 73–74
Comer, Shawn, 189
Commitments, 157
    fulfilling, 104
Community, building your, 190–191
Community engagement, 69
Competition, 34
    actions of, 95
Confidence, 85
    inspiring, 67
Confirmation
    asking for, 62
    in creating dialogue, 114–115
Connections
    creating through values, 171–173
    maintaining, 55–56
Consistency of quality, 143
Consumer choices, decision fatigue and, 139
Content, framing and content strategy,
    154–155, 158–159
Context, setting the, 153
Conversation, situating, in creating dialogue,
    115–116
Coping mechanism, 12
Core purposes, 6
Core values, 6, 9, 10
    of sustainable businesses, 10–11
    upholding, 16
Correction
    asking for, 62

in creating dialogue, 114–115
Counter-examples, soliciting, 62
Creativity
    encouraging, 67
    importance of, to SAS, 99
Credit, watching your, 94
Crisis, critical thinking during, 68–69
Critical thinking
    achieving purpose through refined,
        67–78
    during a crisis, 68–69
    versus emotionally driven decision-
        making, 77–78
    honing of skills in, 65–66
    promises and, 70–71
    pursuing purpose through, 57–66
Crocs, 112
Cross-pollination programs, 109
Cross-training, 109
Crowd sourcing, 175
Culture
    bottom-up approach to, 28
    building flourishing, around your
        values, 105–119
    changing the, 102–104
    creating robust company, 90
    defined, 28, 91
    shared values of, 91–104
    top-down approach to, 28–29
Customer-centricity, 80
Customer service, commitment to
    exceptional, 144

D

Davey, John, 92–93, 98
Davey, Martin, 93
Davey Tree Expert Company, 92–98
Deception, 25
Decision fatigue, 138–140
Decision making
    critical thinking versus emotionally
        driven, 77–78
    ego-driven, 73
    values, emotions and, 128–136
Decisions
    justifying, 71–72
    knowledge as critical to making good, 71
    making, that impact business, 67
Deming, Deborah, 159–160

Design experience idea, 142
Details, burdening yourself with, 96
Development of expertise, 63–65
deviantART, 183
de Waal, Frans, 146–147
Dialogue
    assumptions in creating, 116
    confirmation or correction in, 114–115
    continuous, 117
    creating, 113–116
    listening in creating, 113–114
    situation of conversation in creating,
        115–116
Diligence, 97
Direct mail, 186–187
Disagreement, 116–117
Divine command theory, 35
DIY, 53
Doubt, handling, 95
Due diligence, 77
Duty, 95
    in justification of decisions, 72
Duty-based ethics, 35

E

Economic success, shared values and, 162
Edison, Thomas, 176
Edison General Electric, 176
Ego-driven decision making, 73
Einstein, Albert, 15, 139
Electronic media, 187
Ells, Steve, 122–123, 162
Emerging responsibilities, 128–129
Emotional connections, in branding, 147
Emotional core of values, 144–145
Emotionally driven decision-making, versus
    critical thinking, 77–78
Emotions, decision-making, values and,
    128–136
Empathy
    altruism and, 146
    as genetic inheritance, 145–147
    human capacity for, 12
Employees
    advocacy for, 69
    finding and keeping, 155
    listening to, 86
    making good, 94
    treating as human beings, 94
    valuing, 98–99
Employee stock ownership program (ESOP),
    93
Employers
    alignment of career goals with, 80
    being appreciated or values by, 80
Enron scandal, 9
Environmental sustainability, 69
Excellence, devotion to, 104
Expenses, watching, 94
Expertise, development of, 63–65

F

Facebook, 111–112, 183, 189
    key to success on, 190–191
Fairness, concept of, 147–148
FedEx, 140, 142, 144, 172, 176
Financial profit
    belief in, 193
    as goal of business ventures, 11
Flatterers, being wary of, 96
Flickr, 183
Focus groups, 73–74, 76
Food truck industry, success of, 176–177
Ford Motor, 140, 143, 144
Framework, providing a, 153
Franklin, Benjamin, 182
Friendliness, 97
Fritidsresor, 129

G

Gale, Porter, 165
Gandhi, Mahatma, 121
Gates, Bill, 106
Gekko, Gordon, 12–13
General Motors, 176
    automobile recall policy of, 9
Genetic inheritance, empathy as, 145–147
Gimmicks, 144, 172
Gladwell, Malcolm, 177
Good, defined, 22
Goodnight, Jim, 98–99
Goodwin, Doris Kearns, 82
Google search, 175
Gordon, Jeff, 185
Great Depression, 176
Great Recession, 175, 176
Greed, as value, 12
Groupon, 176

Guiding principle of action, defining value as a, 22

H

Happiness, as tangible, 141–142
Harquail, CV, 156
Help, asking for, 191–192
Hierarchial structure, decline of, 174
Honesty, 25
Honing of critical thinking skills, 65–66
HP, 168
Human beings
    respect for other, 25
    treating employees as, 94
Human beings, capacity for empathy, 12
Humanity, respect for, 10
Humble, staying, 53
Hush Puppies, 177–178
Hyatt Hotels, 176

I

IBM, 176
Ideas
    giving a try, 116–117
    reasons for going viral, 181–182
Individual responsibility, value of, 102
Individual values, connection between business values and, 27–28
Information as 24/7, 138
Information responsibility, 69
Innovation, 104
Instagram, 183
Integrity, 104
Intrigue, 169–171
    accidental creation of, 177
    creating, in promoting purpose, 165–178
    superficial, 169
    sustainable, 170–171
Iron Mountains, Inc., 68–69
Irons, Wayne, 3

J

Jobs, Steve, 106, 133–134, 177
Joplin, Missouri, multiple vortex tornado in, 68–69
Judicial rulings, decision fatigue and, 139
Jungle, seeing the, 138
Just do it attitude, 143
Justification

of decisions, 71–72
of values, 36–42

K

Kant, Immanuel, 179
Kim, Jack, 175
Kimane, Emma, 151
Knaust, Herman, 68–69
Knowledge, as critical to making good decisions, 71

L

Labovitz, George, 115–116
Leaders
    challenging ego of, 85
    components of great, 84
    essence of, 100–101
    line walked by, 73
Learning, performance and, 128
Lennox International, 73
Lexmark, 168
Limbic system, 147
Lincoln, Abraham, cabinet of, 82–84
Linked In, 183, 189
Listening, 62, 86, 113–116
Lived experience, 75
Logical relations, identifying, 75
Long-term engagement, formula for sustaining, 108
Los Angeles, success of food truck industry in, 176–177
Lundgren, Johan, 129

M

Magic moments, 54–55
Management of change, 117–119
Margolis, Joshua, 128–129, 130
Marketing, vertical, 169
Mayer, Marissa, 107–108
McFee, Joseph, 171
Meaney, William, 68
Meaning, 50–52
Meaningful experience, 140–144
Mehiel, Dennis, 99–102, 134
Message, making yours matter, 182
Microsoft, 176
Mindshare Marketing Group, 189
Morale, keeping up, 100
Morality, 28

origin of, 146
Moran, Monty, 122–123
M&T Bank, 50–52
Multiple vortex tornado in Joplin, Missouri, 68–69
Mycoskie, Blake, 134–135

N

New Coke, rollout of, 73–74
New York City, word of mouth marketing in, 177–178
Niemüller, Martin, 105
Nike, 140
No-blind-transfer policy, 51
Nordstrom, 141, 144

O

Obama, Barack, 43
Okidata, 168–169
Online experiences, as personal, 141
Opportunity, difference between risk and, 67
Organization, commitment to environmental and social responsibility, 134
Organized reasoning, importance of, 74–77

P

Panic of 1907, 176
Patagonia, 148–149
People
    fear of speaking their minds, 84–85
    finding, who matter, 190
    getting, on board, 152–160
    surrounding yourself with compatible, 79–90
Perfection, working toward, 97–98
Performance, learning and, 128
Personal improvement, 50–52
Pinterest, 183
Pioneer Basement Waterproofing, 57–58
Plato, 33
Post-recession growth cycles, length of, 175
Poverty, short-term decision-making and, 139
Presentation, focusing on your, 153–155
Primal Leadership (Goleman), 86
Print media, 186
Profits
    financial, 11, 193
    making reasonable, 95
    in measuring success, 52

Promises, 52
    fulfilling, 104
    as promises, 70–71
Psychological power of beliefs, 49
Purpose(s)
    achieving, through refined critical thinking, 67–78
    achieving your, 121–136
    aligning values and, 123–124
    beliefs on action, as meaningful, 137
    creating intrigue in promoting, 165–178
    derailed, 124–126
    involving others in your, 137–149
    methods of achieving your, 151–163
    pursuing, through critical thinking, 57–66
    sense of, 9
    supporting, 62
    surrounding yourself with people who believe in your, 79–90
    uncovering your, 43–56

Q

Quality, consistency of, 143

R

Radio, 187
Reach, 186
Reasoning, importance of organized, 74–77
Recessions, 175, 176
Recidivism, 166
Relativism, questions of, 36
Relevance, 50–52
Religion, 28
Rephrasing, 62
Reputation, building, 113–114
Resistance to change, 118
Respect, 104
    deserving, 96
    for other human beings, 25
Responsibility
    in promoting accountability, 110–113
    value of individual, 102
    Responsibility gap, 128–129, 130
Revlon Cosmetics, 176
Risk, difference between opportunity and, 67
Roosevelt, Eleanor, 110
Rosansky, Victor, 115–116
Rushkoff, Douglas, 111–112

S

Safe and Sound with Amaya, 4–5, 170
 First Annual Butterfly Release associated
  with, 160
Sales representatives, money made by, 94
Salvation Army, 171
SAS, 98–99
 importance of creativity to, 99
Schmidt, Howard, 73, 102–104
Schultz, Howard, 28, 143
The Scotts Company, 169
Self-generated e-mail lists, 190
Self-interest, 97
Selfishness, 97
Self-pity, 181
Self-reflection, 16
Selling process, emotional component of
 the, 153–154
Seward, William H., 82, 83
Sexual harassment, 25–27
Shared values, 161, 162
case study for, 81–82
of a culture, 91–104
Sheahan, Casey, 149
Short-term decision-making, poverty and, 139
Silo effect, 12
Skills, supporting, developing and honing
 your, 60–66
Sobiech, Zach, 188–189
Social justice, 149
Social media, 183–184, 187–192
Social networking, emergence of, 175
Socrates, 14
Southwest Airlines, 141, 144
Speak their minds
 fear of people who, 84–85
 surrounding yourself with people who,
  79–90
Stakeholders, in creating culture, 107–110
Stalemates, 116–117
Starbucks, 28, 140, 143
Stewart, Potter, 21
Story, making yours matter, 189–190
Strauss, Steve, 27–28
Success
 defining in terms of values, 15–19
 factors in, 18
 profits in measuring, 52

SuccessCast, 99
Superficial intrigue, 169
Supporting your purpose, 62
Sustainable businesses, core values of, 10–11
Sustainable intrigue, 170–171

T

Tabulating Machine Company, 176
Target, 140, 142
A Team of Rivals: The Political Genius of
 Abraham Lincoln (Goodwin), 82–84
Technology, advances in, 111–112, 147
Television, 187
Territory managers, 153–155
Time, as crucial to good deliberation, 96
Toddlers, killing of, by preventable
 accidents, 3–4
Tollhouse Cookies, 176
TOMS Shoes, 28, 134–135
 values, purposes and action grid for, 136
Top-down approach to culture, 28–29
Top Ten experiences, characteristics of,
 140–141
Traditional media, 185–187
Transparency, creation of, in workplace,
 112–113
Trustworthiness, 143
Tumblr, 183
Twitter, 183, 189, 191

U

Ultimate customer experience, 55
United States Postal Service, origins of,
 182–183
U.S. Corrugated, 99
U.S. Display Group, 99–102, 134
 values, purposes and action grid for, 136
Utilitarian ethics, 35

V

Values
 alignment purposes and, 123–124
 building flourishing culture around
  your, 105–119
 business, 27–29, 89–90, 132
 case study in defining, 29–31
 creating connections through, 171–173
 decision-making, emotions and,
  128–136

defining as guiding principle of action, 22
defining success in terms of, 15–19
determining source of, 33–42
in driving purpose, 43–56
emotional core of, 144–145
emotionally committed to, 78
greed as a, 12
identifying your, 21–31
of individual responsibility, 102
as intriguing, 174
justifying, 36–42
origin of, 34–36
relationship business and, 119
seeing good and bad, 87
sharing your, 80–81
supporting your, 121–136
surrounding yourself with people who share your, 79–90
tips for making relevant, 52–56
you as the heart of, 106
Values and purpose grid, 135–136, 163
Values-driven activities, 149, 152–160
Values-in-action case study, 18–19

Vertical marketing, 169
Virtue ethics, 35
Vlasic pickles, 127
Voltaire, 79

W

Wall Street, listening to, 86
Walmart, 126–128
    corporate motto of, 126
Walt Disney Productions, 176
Walton, Sam, 126–128
West Jet, 172
Winning, 54
    identifying approaches, 161–162
Word, making yours good, 93
Workplace, creating transparency in, 112–113

Y

Yahoo, 107–108
Yelp, 183, 184
Yes men in Lincoln's cabinet, 82–84
Yousafzi, Malala, 17
YouTube, 183

ABOUT THE AUTHOR

In his thirty-plus-year career, Scott Deming has owned businesses, held board positions, and worked with small, independently owned companies as well as multinational corporations. An expert in employee relationships and customer experience, and author of *The Brand Who Cried Wolf*—an entertaining look at emotional brand building—Deming leads programs for business owners, CEOs, managers, and salespeople across the globe in just about every industry, teaching them the real process for increasing customer evangelism and lasting customer loyalty.